Expel
SPEAKING

Engaging icebreakers, energisers & games

JACKIEBARRIE

Also by Jackie Barrie

The Little Fish Guide to Writing Your Own Website (2013)
The Little Fish Guide to Networking (2011)
The Little Fish Guide to DIY Marketing (2010)

Published by Comms Plus
ISBN 978-0-9565933-6-8

Jackie Barrie T/A Comms Plus
86 Belmont Road Beckenham Kent BR3 4HL

Experientialspeaking.co.uk | JackieBarrie.com

Reviews

"Whenever I need to include a new interactive exercise in one of my presentations, I pick up the phone to Jackie Barrie. I have used a number of her creative inspirations and they always have the right balance of engagement, humour and making a key point. This book will be a tremendous resource for any trainer looking to enthuse and engage with their participants."
Andy Lopata, Business Networking Strategist
Recipient of the Professional Speaking Association Award of Excellence (PSAE)

"Jackie is an expert at thinking of and helping the development of fun, impactful breakout activities for use in a keynote."
Rob Lilwall
Global adventurer, author and speaker

"Jackie's book is so full of creative ideas to engage groups, they will drop their phones, pay attention and want to play! Great book, easy to use, brilliant ideas! Bravo Jackie!"
Shelle Rose Charvet
Author of Words That Change Minds

"Jackie is able to keep the full attention of the audience with a range of audience participation activities."
Alan Timms
Santander UK Corporate & Commercial

"Jackie is expert at communicating in a way that audiences respond to and act on."
Steve Morris
Freemans PLC

"If icebreakers and energisers are part of your world, Jackie will provide you with practical ideas that work."
Ges Ray
Founder, Speaking in Public and builder of confidence in your public speaking

"I've been a facilitator for 12 to 13 years and it's always refreshing to learn new tools. I think I had only seen one variation of these before. So these are brand new tools that I can definitely use in my workshops."
Robin Levesque
Author, speaker, trainer

"I love every single activity. Even the ones I've maybe seen before, she puts a different spin on that makes it more interesting. I can definitely see how I'm going to use a bunch of these in the workshops and presentations I do."
Diane Rolston
Coach, speaker, author, mentor

"Jackie's got a lot of ideas that I will definitely use in my keynote and workshops."
Lowry Olafson
Performing songwriter, speaker, workshop leader

Event organiser comments

"Jackie was a speaker at our inaugural Inspire Recruitment event. In short she 'nailed it'. She took a potentially boring subject and made it interesting and exciting for the audience. Her delivery style showed not only her ability to engage a crowd but her commitment to tailoring her presentation to the audience."
Alex Moyle

"Jackie can energise an audience and make networking sessions fun and informative. If you need an energy injection during your conference I would highly recommend Jackie Barrie."
Janice B Gordon on LinkedIn

"Excellent and spot on for our crowd. That was one of the buzziest nights we've had and that was down to your injection of energy."
David Gordon
Chair, Young Directors' Forum, IoD

"I expected it to be good and wasn't disappointed. I particularly liked the paper-tearing exercise."
Huw Williams
Croydon Ecademy

Delegate comments

"I started off glazed over but must say after a few minutes I was very interested in the course and at the end wished it was longer. Thank you."
Joy Bamford

"I was impressed by Jackie's approach to teaching – she clearly considers different styles of learning, and I felt the benefit of that. All day, I was completely engaged in the course – no clock-watching whatsoever! As the day went on, I got more excited each time we were set a new task! They were really interesting, enjoyable activities."
Olivia Webb

"Jackie's presentation was highly informative and engaging. The whole audience joined in with the interactive parts. Jackie bubbles with ideas and we all left on a high. She got the standing ovation she deserved!"
Jo Hailey

"I love Jackie's audience participation activities. I could do them all day long."
Alison Charles

Contents

*"I see and I forget.
I hear and I remember.
I do and I understand."*
Accredited to Confucius, Native Americans & the Ancient Greeks
(among others)

Two forewords?

This book encourages you to be creative. Original. To think differently about how you present information to your audiences.

In that vein, unlike most books, it has two forewords instead of one. Both are written by acclaimed international speakers.

The first is by David Gouthro, who's written about experiential learning in general. The second is by Alan Stevens, who's written about icebreakers in particular.

Their words add fascinating perspectives to the book, and I thank them for their kind support.

Foreword: David Gouthro

I remember it clearly. It was the spring of 1981. I was registered to attend the annual NSPI* conference in Montréal, Québec, Canada. Sitting in a pre-conference workshop presented by Sivasailam Thiagarajan (better known as Thiagi), I was exposed to experiential learning activities for the first time.

I was mesmerized. I was hooked – immediately and permanently!

I discovered that getting people **actively** involved in their learning increased their interest, engagement, enjoyment and retention of content. It also increased the likelihood of their learning transferring back on the job... which meant greater perceived value and increased requests to have me back!

For almost 40 years, I have looked for every possible opportunity to meaningfully integrate experiential learning activities into my client work. Whether in a keynote presentation, training course, hosted panel conversation or facilitated meeting, I find people learn more, remember more and are much more likely to do something with the information they've acquired if there are more parts of their bodies taking in the content than just their eyes and ears!

You hold in your hands an amazing collection of tools that any speaker can use to increase the impact and value they bring to their audiences.

The need to use experiential activities is embedded into my DNA and as such, I am always on the lookout for new and better ways to engage the audiences of my clients. To my great pleasure and surprise, I discovered that of 27 activities described by Jackie, 22 were ones I had never seen before – and that is after 40 years using experiential learning activities in my business!

There are several elements in *Experiential Speaking* that I particularly appreciate; that I believe distinguish it from other books of activities.

First, in the Introduction, Jackie provides a wealth of insight, context and advice about why and how to use games and activities. For example, the insistence that a game or activity must have a point will save new 'users' a great deal of grief in their early experiments into experiential learning – especially with more senior or skeptical groups!

Second, I love the way Jackie describes the before, during and after aspects of the exercises. And in the spirit of 'one size fits all... fits none', she describes variations of the activities which should encourage readers to feel free to perform their own experiments.

Third, real-life video examples accompanying many of the activities make it easier for me (and others!) to imagine what it might look like if I was delivering it myself – thereby increasing my willingness to build one or two into my own workshops or presentations.

Another unique feature is found at the end of each activity where Jackie reveals their source. I found reading these notes added a lot of interest for me and spoke to Jackie's integrity. There are too many authors who are happy to imply they are the inventors of certain activities when in fact most are modifications or iterations of something already out there in the public domain.

Do I like Jackie's book? Nope. I love it – for the reasons above and many more.

I must offer a word of caution, though.

After reading the descriptions of the activities and learning through Jackie's experience of using them, you too may become hooked! And, as long as these activities are used in ways that are relevant, add impact and value to your client and audience experiences, there is a distinct danger that you will be remembered long after your competitors are forgotten, and thus much more likely to be invited back time and time again!

*Now ISPI—the International Society for Performance Improvement

David Gouthro
President and Founder, The Consulting Edge
Certified Speaking Professional (CSP)
Former National President of the Canadian Association of Professional Speakers (CAPS)
Founder, Vancouver Noseflute Ensemble

Foreword: Alan Stevens

What you hold in your hand will prove to be one of the most valuable resources you have ever encountered. This book is one that will be referred to time and again by trainers, speakers and educators – in fact anyone who speaks to a group of people for any reason. It provides a wealth of material to get over the initial hurdle of starting well – a skill that few of us possess.

Jackie Barrie has been trying and testing these techniques for many years. She knows what works, and has distilled her expertise into these pages. I have been speaking to groups around the world for over forty years, but many of the ideas in this book were new to me, and I am delighted to have the opportunity to endorse them. They all work amazingly well too!

We all know that awful moment when a speaker or trainer says: "Let's go round the room and introduce ourselves". It makes one's heart sink, and drains away any positive energy that was in the room to begin with. The advice in this book will ensure that will never happen again in any group that you speak to. Instead, you will be able to start with an energising exercise that will lead to a very positive atmosphere, with people ready to learn, and ready to enjoy themselves.

Most importantly, these exercises draw people to experience learning, not just receive it. It ensures that learning becomes an active rather than a passive process, and learning outcomes improve if people feel involved.

I guarantee that this book will prove its worth to you many times over. I am delighted that Jackie has written such a practical and valuable guide to experiential speaking. I wish you well with your application of the wisdom in these pages, and I thank Jackie for her superb efforts in creating this wonderful volume.

Alan Stevens
The Media Coach
Fellow of the Professional Speaking Association UK & Ireland
(FPSA)
Global Speaking Fellow
Past President, Global Speakers Federation (GSF)
Co-author of The Exceptional Speaker

Preface

How this book came about

I was founding co-president of the Southeast region of the Professional Speaking Association (PSA) UK & Ireland. In that role, I was often called upon to run an interactive networking session for our members.

I became renowned for using audience participation exercises to increase the level of fun and engagement.

One day, my co-president Barnaby Wynter and PSA member Antoinette Dale Henderson asked me which book I got my ideas from.

"No book," I replied. "I get most of my ideas out of my own brain."

"You must write the book then," they told me.

And here it is.

About the videos

Most chapters link to a brief video demonstration (I suppose this makes the book itself interactive).

Most of them are only one or two minutes long, and they'll give you instant insights about how to run each activity. You'll also be able to see the audience response, hear their laughter, and witness the buzz that's generated in the room.

They were filmed at events for professional speakers in the UK and Canada. (That's because it's harder to invite a videographer into private events where I've run these activities for clients.)

Capturing and compiling all the videos is one of the reasons it took me so long to complete the book – I wasn't working on it constantly, but it took about two years.

I think they add a lot of value by making each exercise clearer. I hope you agree, and urge you to watch them if you're planning to try any of the activities for your own audience.

Jackie Barrie
Author
Speaker & trainer at JackieBarrie.com
Copywriter at WritingWithoutWaffle.com
Founding co-President of the Southeast region of the Professional Speaking Association UK & Ireland (PSA)

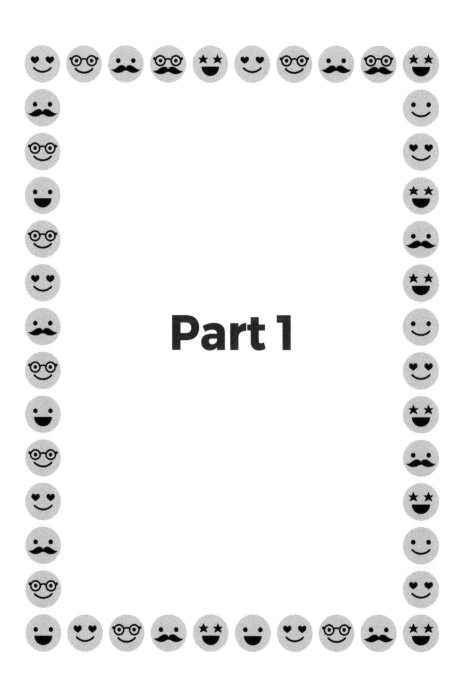

Part 1

Introduction

"For the things we have to learn before we can do them,
we learn by doing them."
Aristotle

Setting the context

I once had to follow the worst speaker I ever saw. By the time he was ready to go on stage, the projector had gone to sleep. He didn't know how to wake it up and I had to whisper instructions to him from the wings.

He started by apologising: "Sorry, this is going to be boring".

He was right.

His slides comprised a three-page Word document in 12pt Arial which he read off the screen with his back to the audience.

But people are polite. They just sat there and took it. They might have day-dreamed a bit, but no-one walked out.

That said, I could sense their relief when he finished and I came bouncing on stage with a high-energy practical session that used no slides (it was about how to make your exhibition stand outstanding, in case you're interested).

Good trainers have been using icebreakers and energisers for decades – and there is a huge range of books they can turn to for inspiration. As far as I can tell, this is the first such book designed primarily for speakers, facilitators and presenters.

There are many keynote speakers who perform on the main stage at conferences around the world. They use platform skills including structure, content and delivery to inform and entertain. Meanwhile, the people in the audience sit quietly (hopefully) to listen and learn.

There are also keynote speakers who tell jokes, or do magic tricks, or play the drums. They are experiential speakers – but we don't all have that kind of talent. The activities in this book are things that **any** speaker can do to be more engaging.

Either way, full-time keynote speakers are a minority in the speaking profession. The vast majority of us speak to smaller groups in a training room setting. And even the most famous keynoters may also provide breakouts, workshops and seminars as part of their service.

In a smaller environment, delegates expect a lot more interaction – and it takes a wholly different skillset to deliver this.

By the way, you can even add interaction in a book, by using a flowchart like this:

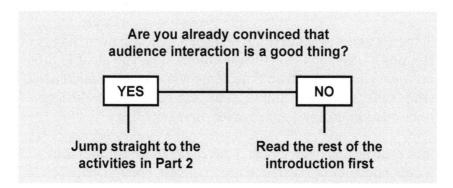

Why audience participation?

We're not only speakers and trainers. Sometimes we are audience members too. And we know what it feels like to miss out when we'd prefer to be involved.

For example, I like to go to Midnight Mass on Christmas Eve. The Mass is usually preceded by a carol service made up of bible readings alternating with hymns sung by the choir and traditional carols sung by the congregation. I always get excited to see what carols we're due to sing, and flip through the hymn book in advance in anticipation.

Last year, I was disappointed to see that one of the congregation carols was a song that I didn't know. When we got to that point in the service, it turned out that no one else in the congregation knew it either, leaving only the choir to sing along.

"That's not fair," I thought. "I wanted to do my bit towards the singing, and now I can't".

That story shows how willing people are to interact, and how disappointing it can be when we're not allowed to.

Some speakers seem to think that asking for a show of hands or running a Q&A session counts as interaction. The ideas in this book go a lot further than that. Some work for huge audiences, while others are more suited to small groups. All are designed to be adapted to suit your own learning outcomes.

As a professional copywriter, I am reluctant to admit it. But words on paper or on screen aren't always enough. Even explaining things verbally, face-to-face, won't do the trick every time. Sometimes, the best way to get your message across is through an activity that your audience undertakes.

This book includes many of the tried-and-tested games, icebreakers and energisers I have used through the years as a trainer and speaker. It also includes some of the best activities run by other people that I've experienced as a delegate and audience member (included with their permission, wherever I've managed to track them down).

As you'll see when you watch the videos, the audience has fun – but it's important to recognise that the activities are not **just** for fun. They are all intended to help you get your message across in a more memorable way.

This next story proves the point.

A little story

You'll find a paper-tearing exercise in the Miscellaneous section (p202). A year or so after doing it at a PSA Southeast event, I went back and asked the audience if they remembered it. They did. I asked them if they also remembered the lesson it was intended to impart. After a moment of thought, they did. And then I asked if they remembered a single thing I'd said. They didn't. And neither did I.

The point of that anecdote is that people remember experiences they had more than they remember anything they heard or saw. So if you want them to remember your message, it's wise to give them an unforgettable experience that anchors it in their mind.

Experience economy

Everything changes.

After the agrarian, industrial and digital economies, we're now in the 'experience economy' – an expression first coined in 1998 by Pine and Gilmore. They argued that businesses must orchestrate memorable events for their customers, and charge for the value of the transformation that they provide.

As you may have noticed, the 'experience' trend is big in marketing at the moment, and traditional retailers who don't provide a good customer experience are dying off right, left and centre.

For speakers and trainers, our career depends on the experience we give our audience.

Experiential learning

You might have heard of the Cone of Learning that evolved from research by Edgar Gale in the 1960s, as shown in the graphic below.

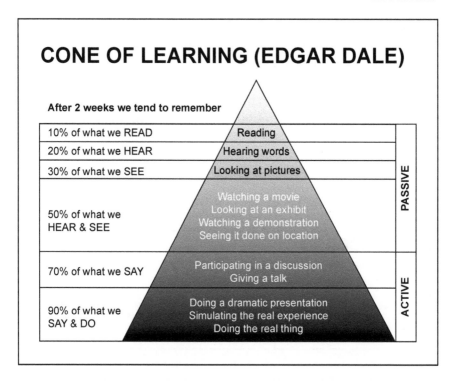

The model is also claimed by the National Training Laboratory, and is sometimes called the Cone of Experience or Pyramid of Learning. It led to a theory of 'experiential learning', sometimes called 'action learning'.

Common sense tells you that the order of activities might be about right, but the specific percentages are rather too convenient to be true. (In fact, Dale didn't include any numbers on his original continuum.)

Today, it's known that memory and recall are dependent on many other variants as well as the style of learning.

However, good trainers have always known that less is more. The less lecturing you do, and the more you make the participants do, they more they learn.

As well as experiential learning, there is another trend that most of these activities tap into. It's called gamification.

Gamification

This screenshot shows the definition from Google:

> # gamification
> /ˌɡeɪmɪfɪˈkeɪʃ(ə)n/ ◀⟩
>
> *noun*
>
> the application of typical elements of game playing (e.g. point scoring, competition with others, rules of play) to other areas of activity, typically as an online marketing technique to encourage engagement with a product or service.
> "gamification is exciting because it promises to make the hard stuff in life fun"

In effect, the activities in this book are a way to gamify the messages you deliver in your workshops and presentations, in order to encourage engagement and give your audience an experience they'll remember.

Case study

One of my trainees ran a security company, and considered that he'd done all the marketing he possibly could. We came up with the idea of adding a game on his website, with a factory floorplan. Site visitors could drag icons of fire alarms and burglar alarms onto the floorplan to protect the building. If they got it right, they got a congratulatory message. But if they got it wrong, animated fires would break out, cartoon burglars would break in, and potential customers would get the message that perhaps the security firm knew more about protecting buildings than they did – because a soft-sell approach sometimes works better than a hard-sell advert.

Inspiration

As you may notice, my inspiration often comes from traditional parlour games, board games and TV shows. Like games, the activities often include elements of playfulness, competition and reward.

If you go to a show that you find particularly entertaining or memorable, analyse how the performer achieved that. What ideas does it generate for you? How can you adjust them for your own learning outcomes?

Millennials

It could be argued that gamification works particularly well with so-called millennials, commonly defined as people born between 1981 and 2000. It's difficult to generalise about individuals, but this age group are now the largest segment of the workplace. They grew up with computer games. Allegedly, their brains work faster, and they're good at multi-tasking.

The world of work and education is therefore incorporating more and more gamification to accommodate their needs and expectations.

For example, Quest to Learn is a New York school that's centred around game-based learning, in an attempt to make education more relevant and engaging for modern children. Their educational philosophy was developed by top educators and game theorists at The Institute of Play, with funding from The MacArthur Foundation.

Badgeville.com (now SAP Sales Cloud) uses gamification to motivate sales teams. They surveyed over 500 people, ranging from entry-level employees to C-level executives, looking at the success of gamification across US organisations.

They found that 78% of workers were using games-based motivation at work and nearly all respondents (91%) said these systems increased their engagement, awareness and productivity. Across all generations, 72% believed that gamification would inspire them to work harder.

Not surprisingly, younger generations have greater expectations. Nearly three-quarters of survey respondents aged 22-35 said gamification should be "expected" in a modern organisation, whereas a little over half of those aged 36-55 years shared that outlook.

Speakers and trainers who are booked to educate and inspire millennials need to be aware that they demand more from us. We can't give them information in the same way it was given to us (especially if we're older than them), otherwise they'll be disengaged and we'll be seen as outdated and irrelevant.

Here are a couple of stories to illustrate this in practice.

Case studies

I was training an in-house marketing team in copywriting skills. They were all in their twenties. Both the HR representative and their manager warned me I'd have a hard time keeping attendees off their mobile devices during the course. By using many of the techniques in this book, it meant they had to put away their phones, tablets and laptops. Afterwards, they gave great feedback about how engaged they were throughout the day, and the company asked me back to train two more of their teams.

Similarly, I run a regular Copywriting for Recruitment masterclass with recruiter, Mitch Sullivan. One of the things I do is give out Smarties when delegates write anything smart, and mini-Babybels when they write something cheesy. At the end of the day, the person who's written the best or most improved ad (as voted by the other delegates) wins a bottle of Prosecco.

Of course, not everything always works perfectly, so here's a confession.

Most people take this in good humour. They all want Smarties, and some even compete to win cheese. Only one attendee has ever complained (out of about 500 we've trained so far) because she felt humiliated by being given cheese. Another accidentally ate the red wax wrapping around the Babybel and spent the coffee break Googling: "Will I die from eating wax?"

Note that chocolates and cheese don't work as prizes if you're working with a roomful of vegans, which happened to us once in Brighton. For them, we might print out green cards reading 'congratulations' or 'well done', and red cards saying 'oops' or 'must try harder'.

To avoid a negative reaction, it's important to set it up correctly at the start of the day. I try to soften any negative feedback by saying things like: "I can tell that your instincts are absolutely right, but you've quite understandably fallen into bad writing habits because you've seen a million job ads written that way."

We also make sure to award cheese to each other if we say something cheesy. It makes the experience more inclusive, and attendees love it when we make a mistake or we're self-deprecating.

We stick with it because it works. It's an engaging way to help delegates understand the point we're trying to make about their writing. Smarties and Babybels have also become a bit of a theme when we mention the course on LinkedIn, which is where we primarily promote it.

I don't much like being judgemental, acting like an English teacher that might remind delegates too much of school, or playing the 'good cop, bad cop' routine. So I wondered whether getting attendees to decide whether the others deserved Smarties or cheese would work better. We tried it once, but found they all looked to us, the trainers, to see which way we were voting. On reflection, they had paid money for us to teach them new skills, so it is important for us to be the ones who take responsibility for guiding them the right way.

Engaging audiences

With experiential learning and gamification in mind, it's no surprise that people are going off the chalk-and-talk type of lecture that many of us became accustomed to at school.

Today's theatre audiences don't want to sit in passive admiration while the performance happens on stage. Paying audiences want to be engaged. And they vote with their money.

As evidence of this, you can often obtain discounted tickets to traditional theatre shows, because they can't sell them at full price. For example, I got top seats at half price for a *Riverdance* performance that would once have been completely sold out. Even at a reduced price, the theatre was almost empty.

Instead, there is a rise in immersive theatre, where the audience turn up (sometimes in costume), and are led to stand, sit or walk about on the set, in effect acting as extras alongside the performers.

For example, I've been to see the *Great Gatsby* run by Secret Cinema. For this show, audience members are invited to dress up in the style of the day, such as wearing flapper dresses, fishnet tights, and long strings of pearls for the women, and sharp suits for the men.

Before the show, the audience is moved through themed rooms while cast members interact with them. The main action is performed more traditionally in a large central area, with the audience standing around to watch. Between scenes, cast members take small groups aside to participate in separate mini-shows in various side rooms. During the event, there's even the chance to learn the Charleston. I went with some of my dancer friends, and we loved it!

I've also been a 'guest' at *The Fawlty Towers Dining Experience* and *The Wedding Reception*. These interactive shows are partly scripted and partly improvised. They are staged in a hotel where you're served a three-course meal. The cast members interact and ad-lib with individual audience members, while the actual performance happens between the tables in between courses. It's hilarious – and different every time, which tempts people to book again.

Similarly, museums and art galleries used to display their exhibits in simple glass cases and frames. Now, you will find all sorts of activities to attract and engage visitors.

In 2018, I attended an immersive art exhibition at the Atelier des Lumières in Paris. It featured animated artwork by Gustav Klimt projected onto the entire floor and wall area while classical and operatic music played. Instead of viewing the paintings from the outside, it was like being right inside them.

Crowd-pleasers

Audience interaction is not a new idea.

The Proms is an eight-week season of classical music, founded in 1895. Prom is short for promenade concert, because the audience was free to stroll around the pleasure gardens while the orchestra was playing.

Today, the Proms are primarily performed at London's Royal Albert Hall. At the Last Night of the Proms (which many people consider the best bit – it's always a sellout), the audience is expected to wave flags, bob up and down, and join in with singing patriotic songs. It's a fine tradition!

In the same spirit, Dutch violinist, André Rieu is best known for playing classical waltzes at informal comedic shows that have an engaging party atmosphere. He performs with his orchestra worldwide, with shows live-streamed into cinemas and shown on TV.

You may have seen the movie *Bohemian Rhapsody* which won a Golden Globe award for best film drama. The film makes clear how the band, Queen, became the success that they were – it's because their most notable anthems were based around the audience.

In one scene, lead guitarist Bryan May explains an idea where the audience stamps the rhythm, which became the song *We Will Rock You*. *Radio Gaga* has the audience clapping in time, *We are the Champions* has everyone swaying along with their arms in the air, and (thanks to the film *Wayne's World*) everyone knows the right moment to start head-banging to the title song.

I think bands like Queen are so successful – not only because of their musical ability – but also because of the way they play the audience.

Michael Bublé is another performer who loves audience interaction. Between his songs he chats and ad-libs like a standup comedian. You might have seen the viral video from 2013 when he spontaneously invited teenager Sam on stage with him to sing *Feeling Good*. You'll find it on YouTube – here's the link: youtu.be/_cw1uLVSl1Y. It's a wonderful example of Michael's generosity, stagecraft, and control of the show.

I don't know if he was the first, but lots of performers have since created 'singalong' opportunities, both on stage and online.

Even traditional sports are introducing new ways of engaging their audiences. Although my cricket-loving father doesn't approve, the International Cricket Council (ICC) has endorsed 'cricketainment', where, in the Twenty20 version of the game, music is played at key moments for the crowd to sing along.

As speakers and trainers, I realise that most of us aren't required to entertain huge stadiums. The point is that our audiences and trainees are also the audiences at those big shows and events – and that sets their level of expectation. With audiences increasingly expecting to be part of the action, there is a growing need to involve them more in your talks and training sessions too. They don't want to just sit and listen any more. They want to be engaged.

For me, engaging an audience properly goes way beyond requesting a show of hands, asking them to share their thoughts in pairs, or inviting them to tweet quotable quotes.

Engaging individuals

This book includes the activities I use most often. Note that none of them involve expensive props, individual role-play or potential embarrassment. They are more about group interaction and engagement.

Unlike calling for individual volunteers, everyone is in it together. They all participate due to peer pressure. And they find that working in groups creates a shared, bonding experience.

Be aware that some people might be reluctant to engage – maybe because they've had a bad experience in the past, or identify themselves as shy or introverted. Here's how to get around that reaction.

There must be a point

Some people hate any kind of audience participation. Most people (quite rightly) hate pointless audience participation. So there must always be a point. Whichever exercise you use should fit your theme and help meet your training objectives.

People like to know **why** they have to do something. Here's an experiment from 1978 that shows how powerful this is.

Ellen Langer et al looked at what happened when people asked to jump the queue so they could use a busy photocopier. Here are their findings:

- "Excuse me, I have five pages. May I use the Xerox machine?" = 60% compliance
- "Excuse me, I have five pages. May I use the Xerox machine, because I have to make copies?" = 93% compliance
- "Excuse me, I have five pages. May I use the Xerox machine, because I'm in a rush?" = 94% compliance

The difference was the word "because".

It's a powerful word, so it's wise to use or imply it when you explain why you are asking people to do the things you're asking them to.

If you'd like to find out more about the study, search *The Mindlessness of Ostensibly Thoughtful Action.*

Physical activities

I understand why some speakers get their audiences to dance.

It's because, when everyone moves as a group, it creates a psychological sense of one-ness. Think about when you go for a walk or drive your car. You don't say: "I walked about in my clothes" or "My car and I drove round the corner". It's because we self-identify with anything that moves along with us.

Sharing choreographed moves makes us feel like individual parts of a bigger whole. This is why armies march, and why members of choirs and dance troupes often form strong bonds with one another.

For that reason, a physical activity can work when you're trying to build a common culture or fast-track team building.

However, some people hate it. Enforced dancing can be uncomfortable and really awkward – even for those of us who love to dance.

As with any activity, you have to get audience buy-in first.

If people have opted to attend your session, and they know what they're in for, that's fine. But if you try to make an audience dance when they're not expecting it, it just won't work for everyone.

Another example that misses the mark for me is when a speaker asks the audience to cross their arms or clasp their hands together, and then to re-cross them the 'other' way. The point of this exercise is that people fall into the habit of doing things a certain way, and to demonstrate that change feels 'wrong' somehow.

The trouble is, I've seen this done so often that it's lost its impact. Not only that, but I've done a lot of yoga and balanced out both sides so I no longer know which is 'natural' and which is the 'unnatural' state – and I won't be the only person in the audience who's like that.

It can also be awkward when speakers try to conduct a relaxation exercise as part of their talk. They ask the audience to sit squarely with uncrossed legs, rest their hands on their thighs, close their eyes, and take three deep breaths. Then they talk people through a guided visualisation.

I'm perfectly happy to indulge the speaker and go along with it, but probably only because I've done similar things before, through choice. I know from talking to other audience members that they just don't get it. They haven't opted into it. So the exercise doesn't reduce their stress levels; it increases them.

Physical exercises like that only work in the right environment, when people know in advance what to expect.

Here are some examples of physical interaction I've seen that went OK:

- A coach who plays snippets from different music genres in a room where the audience is already standing. They start moving naturally along with the beat. He then prompts a discussion about how each style feels and how it relates to various coaching scenarios
- A former dancer who uses movement to demonstrate learning points
- A comedian who uses entertaining dance routines as part of her show
- A speaker on health and fitness who entices the audience to stand and do a few squats
- A neurologist who tells the audience to make a fist with one hand, and wrap the other hand over it. This emulates the limbic system, with the wrist as the brain stem, the fist as the amygdala (reptilian brain) and the

cerebral cortex overlaid on top. It's more memorable to do it this way than by using a slide with a diagram

Cultural differences

There are cultural differences, of course. Whatever you do has to be right for your audience.

The US TV host, Ellen Degeneres, has her audience dancing in the aisles before the start of her chat show. It works because they know what to expect and they love her enough to join in. I suspect much of her success is because she focuses so much on the audience. What's more, her guests are often ordinary people who've done extraordinary things, rather than a parade of celebrities pushing their latest project. She also gives out prizes and surprises.

In Northern Europe, people are typically more restrained than they are across the Atlantic. In fact, I still remember the shock when I first saw UK audiences whoop and holler on the TV show *The Price is Right*.

Some chat show hosts also run book clubs, such as Oprah Winfrey and Richard & Judy in the UK. They don't just promote book sales, they also engage the audience by inviting them to contribute their opinions.

British comedian Miranda Hart 'broke the fourth wall' at key moments during her TV sitcom *Miranda*. She gives a knowing look to camera while in a scene. Watching on your sofa at home, it's as though she's looking directly at you. In interviews, she explained that she resurrected this style inspired by the late great comedy duo, Morecambe and Wise.

There are so many examples that I bump into them all the time. Remember, the point is that your delegates are living in this cultural context. They are used to this level of interactivity. It's fast becoming the norm.

As I keep stressing, it's all about the audience.

About the activities in this book

You'll notice that most of the exercises in this book are low-tech. At most, they involve pen and paper or card, which should be available in any stationery shop, office or hotel environment.

One advantage is that such props are cheap and easy to buy or borrow on the spot if the originals are lost in transit. Another benefit is that it makes the activities very tactile. Involving more senses means the memory is carved more deeply into the brain – because the more mental processing people have to do, and the more modalities they use, the more likely they are to remember things.

Note that, while the exercises may not require great expense or technology, you might have to invest a bit of time, as some of them do require a bit of preparation.

Some of the exercises also need space, such as a breakout room, separate area, or simply moving the chairs to the sides of the room.

In many cases, I've suggested alternative ideas in the 'variations' section. Do join facebook.com/groups/ ExperientialSpeaking and let me know if you think of any others.

Mind your mindset

To inspire your audience to participate, you must be in the right mindset.

What do you do with games? You play them. Therefore, you need a playful mindset yourself.

To facilitate these exercises effectively, you must love playing games (or fake it really well). You need your own energy to be up if you are going to uplift the energy of your delegates. If you don't have fun, neither will they.

What to say

Sometimes I've suggested dialogue you might use. That's because all these activities have been tried and tested on many occasions, and the same conversations seem to happen every time.

It's to give you an idea about what might typically happen, so you can be prepared and ready to respond in your own way.

Occasionally, I have suggested questions you might ask – but I'm not trying to be too prescriptive. As mentioned in various places throughout this book, the whole point is that you adapt each exercise to meet your own particular needs and learning objectives. That also means saying things in your own way.

Often, I'll set a task 'against the clock'. Telling people there is a short timescale and adding a sense of urgency means they are more likely to stop whatever else they are doing or thinking, and pay attention to you.

There's no such thing as too much clarity

You need to give clear instructions, with high support and low challenge.

I'm a member of a mastermind group – a group of peers who meet regularly to share business challenges, with the aim of generating ideas you wouldn't think of by yourself.

At the beginning of each session, we mark our position on a four-box grid as shown below. This is a simple visual aid that tells the others what level of support and challenge we need that day. It recognises the fact that some days we might feel more wobbly and need 'stroking' and encouragement, while on other days we might feel more robust and open to harder questioning from the others.

It's really useful to refer back to during the masterminding sessions, to ensure we give each member the balance of challenge and support that they need.

When playing these activities with an audience, you don't always get the chance to negotiate this balance.

To be on the safe side, it seems appropriate to give people lots of support and encouragement to start with, and not to push them too far. You can move to high challenge later. It's worth it, because that's where creativity lives.

Either way, you need to be absolutely clear about what they are expected to do, and what will happen next. Otherwise they get confused and it reflects badly on you as the presenter.

Case study

If you can, watch out for anyone who looks as though they want to opt out, and give them that chance.

Before one workshop, I spotted an audience member who was looking very unhappy. I took her aside for a moment to have a quiet word. She explained that she'd heard the session was to be highly interactive, and that she was terrified. She imagined she would be brought to the front for a role-play exercise, and that she would be made to look a fool. She also had some issues at home that were making her feel extra wobbly that day.

To reassure her, I told her exactly what to expect, and that there was absolutely no role-playing involved. I promised not to pick on her or even make eye contact, and gave her permission to sneak out to the loo if she felt uncomfortable at any point. This seemed to help. She immediately became less stressed, and ended up staying for almost the entire presentation.

I understood her concerns. You might not believe it now, but I used to be that scared too.

Years ago, as a lowly copywriter in the corporate world, I was on a presentation skills course run by two actresses. I'd fought to be there. In fact, my boss had said: "What do **you** want presentation skills training for? You'll never have to give a presentation." (He'd be amazed to know that's now two-thirds of my working life.)

Anyway, the trainers had made a list of adjectives on the flipchart, and we were each expected to ask another trainee for a lift home in the style of one of the adjectives.

I was young and shy, and **really** didn't want to do it. I was torn between bursting into tears, running to the loo, or leaving the course entirely. As a result, I felt stuck to my chair, unable to do anything.

By the time everyone else had taken their turn, the only adjective left on the flipchart was 'seductive'. Oh no! I saw that as the worst word of the lot, with the greatest potential for embarrassment.

Somehow – I still don't know how – I did it. I think the potential embarrassment of running away was greater than the risk of staying in the room.

Here's what I did.

I took a deep breath and got up, draped myself across the desk, walked my fingers seductively towards one of the other participants, and said, breathily:

"You know this course is called... Dynamic... Presentations?"

He agreed.

I continued: "Well... why don't you give me a lift home... and we'll see just how... dynamic... we can be."

Everyone laughed, and I learned an important lesson about pretending to be brave even when you're not – because no-one will know you're scared unless you tell them.

The point of those stories is that you can't control the state of everyone in your audience, as they may have things going on in their own life that you know nothing about. You don't have to be their therapist. But you do have a responsibility to make your session as interesting, fun and worthwhile for as many attendees as you can.

Add your own twist

If we all do exactly the same things, there's a chance that some people will experience the same activity on more than one occasion – which defeats the object of trying to be creative and original.

You want your training session or speech to be unique, so I end this introduction with another reminder to adapt the ideas to make them relevant to your topic.

I hope you find this book useful, and welcome your feedback.

"One must learn by doing the thing;
though you think you know it,
you have no certainty until you try."
Sophocles

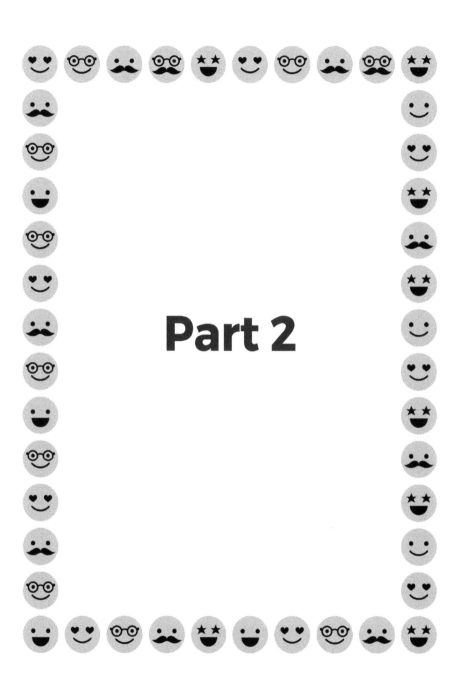

Part 2

Icebreakers

Why you need an icebreaker

The purpose of an icebreaker is to warm up your audience so they are more prepared to listen and learn.

You want to grab their attention from the very beginning.

These icebreakers are not what people expect. This lets them know that their time with you will be different, engaging, and interesting. They can be a useful way for people to get to know each other, and to set expectations for a fun and interesting session – which is exactly the mindset you want your audience to be in.

Getting-to-know-you exercises

Often, a training course starts with a round of introductions. The trainer asks the delegates to introduce themselves in turn, and to share their objectives for the session.

The trouble is, people often refer to this as 'creeping death'. No-one listens to what anyone else says, because they are so worried about what they are going to say themselves.

Some trainers ask each delegate extra questions as well as their names, such as:

- If you were an animal, what would you be and why?
- Tell us two truths and a lie and the rest of us have to guess the lie

- Choose an adjective that describes you and starts with the same initial as your name e.g. Awesome Annie. (That can turn into a memory test when the other delegates are briefed to repeat the chosen names.)
- Give the name of your first pet and the road where you live. This is your 'film star' name

I like to run the introductions in an even more creative and unexpected way than that.

Revision exercises

People tend to remember the first and last thing that happened more than they remember anything you said in the middle.

That's why some of these icebreakers can be used as revision exercises instead. Also, it's important to end your session on a high that reinforces your key points.

In this section

- Snowball fight
- Pig personality profile
- Pass the parcel
- Questions in a hat
- Toilet paper
- Pennies in a basket

Snowball fight

Overview

You can use this as a fun icebreaker or anytime you want to get any message across in a memorable way.

Time

10-20 minutes

Number of people

Works for groups of any size

In advance

Provide each audience member with a blank A4 page or a pre-printed slip of paper with a grid of 140 boxes. Ideally, distribute them in advance of your session. Maybe have a volunteer on standby to hand out extra paper if required.

During the exercise

Tell the audience to write a fascinating fact about themselves, writing one character in each box, including punctuation and spaces. They don't have to fill in every box, but they shouldn't write more than 140 characters.

Tell them it's 140 because that was the number of characters in a tweet before Twitter increased the character count. (It used to be 140 because the original limit for an SMS text message was 160 minus 20 for the username.)

Occasionally, someone will tell you, "I've never written a tweet before" – if relevant, this can lead to a conversation about Twitter, social media, and new beginnings in general.

If anyone looks worried, you'll need to reassure them that it's not a real tweet. It's only a piece of paper that's going in the recycling bin. Their words are not actually going to be live on the internet.

I usually join in the exercise and write my own tweet while they are writing theirs.

As the facilitator, it's interesting to observe people's faces as they participate in this exercise. As this is the first task you have asked them to do, people often concentrate really hard, and worry about what to write.

When I do the activity with freelance journalists (before I train them how to add copywriting to their skillset), they often write a first draft before filling in the piece of paper. They're the only group I've worked with who do this!

If you observe someone hesitating, you can joke that this is the easy bit, and that they don't have to write an essay.

Someone will often say, "There's nothing fascinating about me, I'm really boring".

In this case, you can invite them to write about their favourite film, book or play, or about a family member, or to trust their instincts and write whatever comes to mind.

You might need to nudge the timing along, and say: "30 seconds left" or "Whatever you're writing, you've got ten seconds to finish the sentence".

When you can see that everyone is ready, tell them to screw up the page.

When you ask them to do this, they'll probably look shocked, especially if they have thought hard about what to write. The reason is that we typically think screwed-up paper is rubbish. People don't want to think that about their writing. They are confused because they have obediently obeyed your first instruction and now they think you want them to throw it away.

For this reason, it's important to move quickly on to the next step.

Tell them "We're going to have a snowball fight", and throw your piece of screwed-up paper into the middle of the room. You can add a comment about it being unseasonal (in high summer) or seasonal (in winter).

People will throw their snowballs with greater or lesser energy. Allow the 'fight' to continue for up to three throws – sometimes just one is enough.

Next, tell them to rummage around and pick up the nearest snowball. Note that balled-up paper might have rolled under a chair or into a corner. Ensure everyone gets one.

People will experience a sense of relief as soon they realise their efforts are not unrewarded.

Occasionally, someone will raise a concern because they've picked up their own snowball, and will try to swap it with someone else's. Reassure them that it doesn't matter. Equally, it doesn't matter if they do swap.

Once everyone has picked up a snowball, I start by opening the one I've found, read it aloud, and invite that person to introduce themselves. Sometimes, I take the opportunity to ask them to share what objectives they hope to achieve from the day, and capture those on a flipchart.

Once that person has finished, prompt them to read the snowball they've picked up so the next person can identify and introduce themselves. Repeat until you've gone round everyone in the room.

Ideally, it will make a complete chain, but of course, that doesn't always happen. Sometimes, a sequence of snowballs matches in that Person A reads the snowball of Person B, and Person B reads the snowball of Person A. It's not a problem. You simply go to the person beside them and carry on from there.

After the exercise

On a housekeeping note, during the next break, get someone to gather up all the used snowballs and bin them so the room remains tidy.

Variations

Remember, you need to adapt the exercise according to your topic.

I used to run social media training courses, which is why I asked delegates to write a tweet describing themselves without including their name. It made sense to open a social media course with an icebreaker that involved writing a tweet. Later, I could draw a lesson from it, about social media being social, even when you're on it to discuss business.

When Mitch Sullivan and I train recruiters how to write better recruitment ads, I ask them to write a tweet advertising their own job. This works on many levels. First, it gives us an instant indication of their writing skills. Second, it fits exactly with the theme of the day. Third, it tells everyone in the room what they each do, in a more creative and interesting way than usual.

When I train in-house comms teams how to write compelling copy, I ask them each to complete the sentence 'Copywriting is...' and throw all their snowballs to me. I then read out their definitions (anonymously) and use their responses to guide the course content. It's a really great insight into their level of understanding before we start.

Here's a twist when the group is too big to read out all the snowballs. At a December event with 50 speakers and trainers, I asked each one to write their top tip or learning from the day so far, and then screw the paper up into a ball and throw it round the room before collecting one each. The thinking process served to embed that piece of advice on the memory of the writer, while each reader ended up with one piece of advice to keep as a Christmas gift.

Speaker and workshop facilitator, Stuart Harris, talks about sales and customer service. When he saw this exercise, he suggested yet another twist. At the end of a session, he asks people to write their key learning points in the form of a tweet, and then pins or tacks them all to the wall for everyone to photograph and tweet later on **actual** Twitter.

As a networking activity, you can ask people to write a fascinating fact about themselves (without including their name), screw the paper up and throw it around. Once everyone has picked up a 'snowball', they have to find the person who has written that fact, and talk to them for a couple of minutes to find out more about it.

One summer, I did this with about 40 people in a car park outside a barn just prior to a barbecue lunch. It was a good way of preventing a long queue for the food, because people weren't allowed to leave until they had both found the person who wrote the 'snowball' they picked up, and had been found by whoever picked up theirs.

A final point. You don't have to use paper with pre-printed boxes. You can just use a blank A4 page for each attendee. In that case, you don't need to restrict them to writing 140 characters.

Comments

I suggested this exercise to a speaker who works predominantly in the Far East. Culturally, screwing up paper and throwing it around the room would be very unconventional over there. Being given permission to do something so disruptive would be likely to generate nervous laughter and enjoyment along with compliance. It's another way that this simple activity could be used to lead interesting discussions afterwards.

Source

I first experienced this as an icebreaker on a personal development course when I was in corporate life. The trainer asked us each to write three fascinating facts about ourselves that the other people in the room didn't know. We then had to screw up the paper into a ball, and have a 'snowball fight'. Once we had each picked up a snowball, we had to open the pages in turn, read out the facts, and guess who wrote them.

It was a fun way of finding out interesting things about my colleagues – and it's still stuck in my mind all these years later.

I sometimes used this exercise at networking groups I ran – except that I would only ask them to write one unknown fact. This is how one group discovered that one of their members was pregnant.

The snowball fight idea is adapted from *The Accelerated Learning Handbook* by Dave Meier. In its original form, it's a way of collating questions and checking learning.

Delegates are asked to write a question on a blank piece of A4 paper, screw it up, and throw it to the front. Questions are anonymous so they won't be shy. It adds an element of surprise as you open each one. The trainer can then ask each question in turn for the audience to answer. Alternatively, you can answer the questions yourself.

This technique allows you to keep control. If you open a question that's inappropriate, you can put it aside saying: "Ah, that's too similar to the question before; I've already answered it," or "That will take too long; I'll come back to it" or "I can't read the handwriting on that one". As a further opportunity, you can offer to respond to any unanswered questions in another session, or a followup blog post or webinar.

I shared this suggestion in the Speakers Corner Facebook group when William Roy asked for novel Q&A ideas. After using it, he added this piece of advice:

"The screwed pieces of paper thrown by the audience were a hit, but next time I shall be more precise and say "NO PAPER PLANES!!!!!"

Another way of handling the Q&A session is to give each table a number (if they don't already have one), and to ask each table to prepare a single question they think **other** people might like to ask. Then use a free random number generator app (there are loads you can download from the internet) to decide the order of questions to answer. This idea is courtesy of David Gouthro.

Watch the video

http://tinyurl.com/XPSnowballFight

Pig personality profile

Overview

This icebreaker works especially well with small groups who already know each other. It also works for strangers.

It's particularly relevant when you are going on to run a personal development or personality profiling session, such as Myers Briggs or similar.

I've used it dozens of times, and it never fails to get a laugh.

Time

No more than ten minutes

Number of people

It can be used with groups of any size

In advance

All you need is enough sticky notes to give one to each delegate.

To save time for big groups, it's worth handing out the sticky notes in advance, perhaps by sticking them on the cover of their training manuals, or on an index card, piece of paper or other prop that you will be asking them to use later.

Running the exercise

Ask the delegates to draw a pig on their sticky note.

They will initially be surprised at this request, so reassure them that you are asking them to draw a pig – yes, a farmyard animal. Tell them they do not need to put their name on the drawing, and reassure them that it is not an art competition.

At this point, at least one person will probably say, "That's just as well," or "Thank goodness for that".

Allow a couple of minutes for everyone to complete their drawings. By observing their activity from a distance, you will see when they have finished. If someone is taking an extra-long time, give them a countdown. Tell them there are 30 seconds left, then 20 then 10.

For small groups, invite them to come and stick their sticky notes on a blank flipchart and then gather round to view this pig picture gallery. They will probably laugh and point out various features of the pigs to each other.

For big groups, it's not practical for them to gather round so they should just keep their own drawing on their table or in their lap. They can easily show it to their neighbour if they feel so inclined.

Now, tell them you will interpret the drawings because this is the 'Pig Personality Profile'. You can expect them to laugh when you say this, so allow the laughter to die down before you continue. As I learned on a stand-up comedy course, you never want to tread on a laugh.

It's important to stress that this is just a fun icebreaker, and that people should not read too much into the interpretations. They are not scientifically accurate.

Despite this disclaimer, people are always interested in themselves. They will really want to know what the drawings reveal and decide for themselves whether or not the interpretation is true. They will also enjoy looking at any other pig drawings they can see.

Here is the interpretation according to Google:

- If your pig is drawn towards the top of your paper, you are an optimistic person with a positive attitude

- If your pig is drawn toward the bottom of your paper, you tend to be more pessimistic

- If your pig is drawn toward the middle of your paper, you are a realist who tends to face facts

- If your pig is drawn facing left, you believe in tradition, are friendly and outgoing, and tend to remember dates and birthdays

- If your pig is drawn facing right, you are innovative and active, but less good at remembering dates

- If your pig is drawn facing forward, you are direct, straightforward, welcome discussion, and enjoy playing devil's advocate

- If your pig is drawn with many details, you are analytical, cautious, and may be distrustful

- If your pig is drawn with few details, you are more impulsive, care little for detail and are willing to take risks

- If your pig is drawn with four legs showing, you are secure, stick to your ideals, and can be stubborn

- If your pig is drawn with fewer than four legs showing, you may be insecure, uncertain, or living through a period of major change

- The larger the pig's ears you have drawn, the better listener you are

- And, last but not least, the longer the pig's tail you have drawn, the more satisfied you are with the quality of your sex life!

Depending on how much time you have available, you may need to read out the interpretations quite quickly. This doesn't matter too much, as it's the last line that gets the big laugh. So it's best to pause and slow down at that point.

It helps if you blend innocence and cheeky humour when you deliver the punchline so it doesn't come across as sleazy in any way.

You might get some backchat from people making quips about the length (or shortness) of their pig's tail, so be ready to respond accordingly.

After the exercise

It might be worth reminding them once more that it's just a fun warm-up and that the interpretation isn't necessarily true.

Some people are so proud they will want to show you their drawing afterwards. One person told me he had drawn Donald Trump rather than a farmyard animal. "You told us to draw a pig," he said, "so I did".

One man asked if he could take his pig drawing home to show his wife – I'm not sure why! And when I tell that story after running the exercise, it always gets a laugh.

Variations

You can use blank A4 paper rather than sticky notes (but then, of course, you can't stick the drawings on the wall or flipchart without using pins or Blu Tack or similar).

If you feel that the last line is inappropriate to use for your audience, there are other versions – but they are nowhere near so funny e.g. saying 'social life' instead of 'sex life'. Just type 'Pig Personality Profile' into Google and you will find all kinds of variations.

You can adapt the exercise by getting them to draw something other than a pig and work out your own interpretations to make your point (remember to tell people it's not true or scientific).

This icebreaker is more about entertainment than education, but you might be able to adapt the interpretations to suit your learning objectives.

For example, you can draw out lessons about whether people were embarrassed to share their drawings, and why. Maybe they wrapped their arm around to conceal their drawing from their neighbour, like schoolchildren would in an exam.

If your session is about listening, you can ask whether the interpretation about the pigs' ears was true or not, and start a discussion from there.

Those are just a few ideas. I'm sure you can think of your own.

As stated throughout this book, the intention is not for you to copy each exercise word for word. You should adapt it for your own personality, brand, client, delegates and learning objectives.

Another drawing exercise

I discovered this exercise in corporate life when I was learning about communication skills as part of a management development programme. It's also a parlour game.

Start with a simple drawing, such as a candle, bunch of grapes, or three interconnected geometric shapes (as shown below). Give it to a volunteer, ideally someone who thinks they are a clear communicator.

Without showing the drawing to the audience, your volunteer has to describe what they see in such a way that the audience can reproduce it.

For the drawing above, the volunteer might say:

"Start with your paper in portrait format, that is, with the long edges at the sides and the short edges top and bottom.

Put your pen about one inch in from the left, and about three inches down from the top. You're going to draw a tall rectangle, and your pen is at the top left corner.

Draw a horizontal line about two inches long. At right angles to this, draw a vertical line downwards about five inches long. Draw a horizontal line parallel with the one above, and then draw a final vertical line to close the rectangle.

Next, you're going to draw a circle that intersects with the top right corner of the rectangle. Start with your pen in the middle of the top horizontal line..."

This is a hard exercise. No matter how well the drawing is described, the results created by the audience are unlikely to match the original exactly.

You can use this to draw out lessons about the importance of giving (and following) clear instructions, for example, or about the need to choose the right channel of communication for your message.

A twist on this activity was suggested to me by Scott Johnston when I spoke at PSA Scotland.

Start with an outline drawing. It could be a pig but it doesn't have to be. Draw a 4 x 4 grid over it.

Give the original to your volunteer, and give blank grids to the audience (it will be easier if you label the rows 1, 2, 3, 4 and the columns A, B, C, D).

In this case, the volunteer describes what is in each segment of the drawing, which can assist the audience to reproduce it.

For example, they might start by saying:

> "In the top left box (grid reference A1), you'll draw an open loop. The line starts in the middle of the bottom edge of the box, continues upwards towards the top of the box, and curves round to a 45-degree angle, leaving the box halfway through the right edge..."

The point of this exercise is to talk about the importance of systems and processes, perhaps when introducing a new standard operating procedure, for example.

Group-generated drawings

You'll need three pieces of paper for each participant (and for yourself if you want to join in).

Each piece should be pre-printed with four empty boxes, one above the other, in this order:

- Narrow
- Deep
- Narrow
- Deep

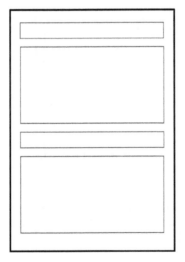

Glue, tape or staple each set of three pages together at the short edges to create a single looooong piece of paper. Fold or roll them, and give one to each participant.

Tell them their first task is to think of their favourite picture, or imagine one. Write the name of the picture in the first narrow box, and then draw it as best they can in the first big box.

Then, ask them to pass their paper to the person on their right.

That person should describe the drawing in the next narrow box, and fold the paper over to hide the picture before passing it to the person on their right.

The next person should read the description. In the next big box, they draw what is described, then fold over the description and pass the paper on.

Keep passing the paper along until all the boxes are filled, then open the pages up and see how the image has been distorted at each stage.

It's likely to produce some hilarious results. You can use it to talk about the danger of assuming the 'cascade' method works for internal communication, for example. I'm sure you can think of other learning points too.

It's hard to trace the original source of all these activities. I was introduced to this particular one at an Applied Improvisation session run by Dave Bourne. He told me he got it from Paul Z Jackson who said he'd learned a version from Liane Fredericks (who no doubt got it from someone else).

More drawing exercises

At an event where I spoke to an audience of landlords, fellow speaker, Sonja Carr, asked people to draw a coffee cup. Most people drew it sideways on – that's what I did with my Starbucks effort on the hotel's dotted notepaper, below.

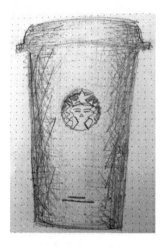

Sonja then showed her own drawing of a cup as seen from above, which looked like a simple circle within a circle. This exercise made a powerful point about creativity, innovation and viewing things from a different angle.

In corporate life, we were asked to draw the company as if it were a vehicle. I remember drawing a snazzy car that had wobbly back wheels to show that it looked good at the front end but that things didn't work very well at the back.

Meanwhile, the boss drew a speeding train with a helicopter hovering above carrying the Board of Directors. The exercise revealed a complete disconnect between the perception held by the leadership team and that of the frontline staff, and gave us the opportunity to address it.

Another idea (inspired by my client, Rose Padfield) is to get people to draw a magazine spread containing pictures and words for an article featuring themselves in five years' time. This could be the start of an interesting session when discussing goal-setting or vision statements, for example.

People have different artistic skills – but it's not about the quality of the drawing. It's about what the exercise means and what they learn from it. The only limit is your imagination...

Source

I was first introduced to the Pig Personality Profile on a now-defunct business networking site called Ecademy. As mentioned, you'll find different versions of it all over Google.

Watch the video

http://tinyurl.com/XPPigPersonalityProfile

Pass the parcel

Overview

This exercise gets people out of their seats and standing up, which is good because moving around increases bloodflow and results in more oxygen to the brain.

You can use it as a getting-to-know-you icebreaker, or as a quirky way of asking revision questions at the end of your training session.

This fun game taps into the child inside all of us. It's certainly an unusual and memorable activity for a business speech or training session.

Imagine the conversation when participants get home.

> *"How was your event?"*
> *"We played pass the parcel!"*
> *"Did you win?"*

It's also a great way of getting to know the people in the room. I find it's especially suitable near Christmas time, a business anniversary, or the birthday of a key individual – but that's not essential for generating a party spirit.

Pass the parcel injects a burst of energy, so it works particularly well just before a break because people then have the chance to continue any conversations that arise.

It brings lots of benefits. For example, it's a random way of allowing various audience members a moment in the spotlight.

Finally, it's a lot of fun. In fact, I've heard people say things like:

> *"This is the best networking I've ever done.*
> *Can we do this all night long?"*

The only downside is that it takes quite a bit of preparation.

Time

10-15 minutes

Number of people

From about 6 to 30

In advance

You will need:

- Index cards – one for each layer of your parcel

- Plenty of giftwrap (ideally in different colours and designs). Alternatively, you can use layers of newspaper or magazine pages

- Selection of retro sweets, because I find that people enjoy the nostalgia of winning a sweet from their childhood. (Every time I've done this, the Curly Wurly bar seems to be particularly popular.) If those are difficult to source, then perhaps use individually wrapped chocolates from a selection box

- Main prize. Something up to the size of a slim paperback means the final parcel will not be too big or heavy. This could be your own book or another one that's relevant to the event

- Copyright-free music (you'll find lots of sources on Google) and / or the appropriate licence to play music in public, or assurance that the venue has this covered

- A way of playing music (loud enough for the audience to hear), and the ability to stop the music mid-way through and start it again. A remote control is ideal

- A room with space for people to form a circle, whether standing or sitting (the 'circle' doesn't have to be perfectly round)

- An empty bin bag to collect the rubbish (because you don't want the client's lasting memory of you being that you left a big mess)

Decide how many layers the parcel will have. Ideally, you need enough layers so that up to a third or even half the people have the chance to win something (if time allows). Let's assume ten. Write a different question on each of ten index cards.

They can be getting-to-know-you questions, business questions, social questions, or fun questions.

Here are some examples:

- *"Who is your favourite client and why?"*
- *"What has been your highlight of the year so far?"*
- *"What are your main hobbies and interests outside work?"*
- *"Who would be at your fantasy dinner party?*
- *"What can you see out of your office window?"*

You could even use questions that reinforce the learning points from your session content.

Wrap up the main prize.

It's nice to add a reward or prize in every layer as well as a question. This acts as a 'thank you' for participating and adds to the energy and banter that results from playing the game. As suggested above, I like to use retro sweets, as this triggers nostalgia and unleashes the child within us all. You might prefer to give away branded USB sticks or another small prize that makes sense for you.

For clarity, use a different wrapping paper for each layer. I like to use wrapping paper in strikingly different colours and designs, so it is very obvious when a layer has been opened. You don't need loads of different designs. Alternating between just two styles is fine.

Add each question and a sweet in separate layers wrapped around the main prize parcel.

If it makes any difference, remember that you'll need to wrap up the final question first, and the first question last (because that's the order they will be opened).

The parcel needs to be well wrapped so it won't fall apart as it's passed around, but it also needs to be easy to open quickly. That means not using too much sticky tape, otherwise people will struggle to open it and that will take too long.

To make the completed parcel look really pretty, I might tie curling ribbon around the outermost layer, but I wouldn't use it on the inside layers as it would take too much time to open.

Note that the final parcel makes a good photo opportunity when you pose with it. The image will be useful for sharing on social media to promote your session before, while it happens and afterwards.

Running the exercise

Tell your audience that you're going to play the traditional children's game of pass the parcel. You might prefer to call it "Pass the Networking Parcel" so they know it's something different to the children's game.

Be sensitive to cultural differences. If you have attendees who didn't grow up with this tradition, you'll need to explain how it works.

Ask the delegates to arrange themselves in a circle. Be sure to take care of any people who can't stand. The game can be played sitting on chairs or even on the floor.

Tell them there will be a question in each layer.

Reassure people that the questions are not trying to test their general knowledge. For example, you are not going to ask them what is 326×17 (assuming that's true, of course). This will probably get a trickle of laughter and comments such as "That's just as well".

Give the parcel to one person to start the game.

During the exercise

If you use your phone to play music through a dock or speakers, make sure you turn off incoming calls and notifications so you're not unexpectedly interrupted. Alternatively, play it through a laptop or tablet with speakers, or get the AV team to play the music for you.

Stand with your back to the audience and start the music. It's important that the participants see that you can't tell where the parcel is when you stop the music, so you do not appear to favour the winners. The game needs to be seen to be fair.

Let the music play for a while, then stop it. It's okay to stop unexpectedly, mid-word or phrase. Switch it up between playing short and long segments of music. You will probably find that you don't play an entire song, even with a parcel that has ten layers to open.

Turn and watch where the parcel has stopped. That person should open the first layer of wrapping, read the question on the card aloud, and answer it. Before they answer, you might have to remind them to read out the question so that everyone else can hear it.

In the spirit of the game, the other people will probably go "Oooh!" when the music stops, comment on the prize that's revealed, and then listen intently to the question and answer.

Depending on their age group, it's fun when people start singing old jingles inspired by any retro sweets you've put in e.g.

> *A Finger of Fudge is just enough...*
> *Toblerone, out on its own...*
> *The Milky Bar Kid is strong and tough...*

Simply allow this to happen and enjoy it. You might like to join in with the singing if you know the words.

Once the winner of that layer has answered the question and any banter has died down, start the music again to continue the game.

To maintain the level of excitement, vary the amount of time the music plays between layers – be sure not to take too long or people will get bored.

Don't worry if people chat to their neighbours while the parcel is going round. The questions, the sweets and the whole experience might trigger memories they want to share. It's not a problem. Remember the objective of the exercise is for people to start conversations i.e. networking.

Don't try to fix it, but ideally, the winners will be more or less evenly spaced around the circle, and the same person will not win too often.

Anticipation will build as more layers are revealed and more questions are answered. Everyone will be wanting to win the main prize in the centre – or, at the very least, they will be curious about what it is.

From the reducing weight and size of the parcel, they will be able to sense when the game is nearing its end.

Once the final prize is revealed, it's likely that people will applaud.

After the exercise

Collect the rubbish (unless that's already been done as you go along).

If anyone gave a particularly interesting answer, you might choose to follow up with them afterwards. Remember, starting conversations is why this is a good exercise to do just before a break.

Variations

I sometimes appoint a helper or request a volunteer to go round with a rubbish bag. They collect the discarded giftwrap paper, index cards and any sweet wrappings while the game is being played.

You can appoint someone to play the role of 'chief sneak' or 'judge'. In case of argument, they can help you adjudicate who the winner is each time the music stops. (I once gave this role to some people who refused to play but were perfectly happy to be observers for me.)

In a small group, you could invite everyone to answer **all** the questions, using each one to promote a longer discussion.

Your questions don't have to be based around getting to know each other. For example, they could be revision questions related to the learning points from your programme, which would certainly be a fun way to close the day.

Another twist is to use forfeits instead of questions in each layer.

Comments

Here are some of the things that might happen so you can be prepared.

You may need to remind players to read the question out loud as well as giving their answer.

If anyone really can't bear the idea of opening a layer, they will shove the parcel on to the next person. There might be a moment of minor protestation, but it will soon be overcome.

If the same person wins twice, they are likely to pass the parcel to the person beside them. It's rather nice that people seem to have an innate sense of fairness. If it's a fit with the theme of your event, you can use those moments to prompt a discussion about that.

Source

Turning this into a networking activity was my own idea. Who would have thought there was so much to say about a child's game such as pass the parcel? But, as you can see, a lot of thought has gone into this – as with all the activities in this book.

Pass the parcel works because it's a childhood ritual. Most of us played it growing up.

As an adult, it has an element of risk, especially if you fear getting a question that you can't (or don't want to) answer. The fear of getting a tricky question is equalled by the excitement about winning the sweets, and the schadenfreude or joy you experience when you see someone else get a tricky question and / or win something.

Watch the video

http://tinyurl.com/XPPassTheParcel

Questions in a hat

Overview

This is another good team-building / getting-to-know-you exercise.

When thinking about new teams, you might find the model below is useful. It was first proposed by Bruce Tuckman in 1965.

He says that all phases are necessary and inevitable for a team to grow, overcome challenges, and deliver results. What you want is to move the group quickly through the model, from **forming** to **storming** to **norming** to **performing**. He went on to add an **Adjourning** phase when the team disbands.

This exercise probably works best at the 'forming' stage, for example, when you have appointed a new committee or project team and the members don't know each other, or they know each other a little bit but not very well. The objective is to fast-track the 'forming to performing' process in a fun way.

It's a great icebreaker on those occasions when conversation feels stilted. What people choose to admit can be very humorous and revealing. It certainly helps teams to bond and get to know each other, and often triggers interesting followup conversations, whether on the same day or in future.

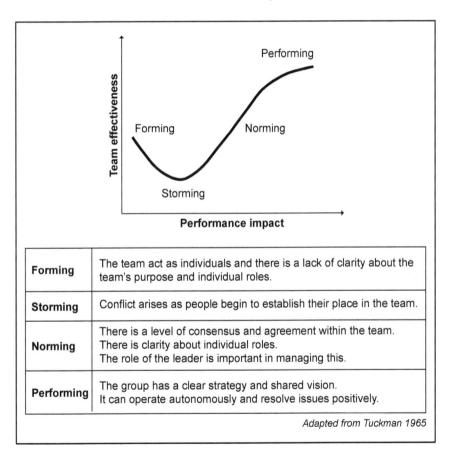

Forming	The team act as individuals and there is a lack of clarity about the team's purpose and individual roles.
Storming	Conflict arises as people begin to establish their place in the team.
Norming	There is a level of consensus and agreement within the team. There is clarity about individual roles. The role of the leader is important in managing this.
Performing	The group has a clear strategy and shared vision. It can operate autonomously and resolve issues positively.

Adapted from Tuckman 1965

Time

10-20 minutes (or more)

Number of people

From 3 or 4 up to about 12

In advance

Fold and tear sheets of blank A4 paper into quarters so you have enough for two, three or four pieces per person. (The only reason I suggest tearing up the paper is to save on waste.)

You will also need a hat, just because they are inherently funny. If it's Christmas, it makes sense to use a festive Christmas hat. Alternatively, you can use a bucket, basket, bowl or any other receptacle.

Each person will also need a pen. With the increased use of smartphones and tablets, some people don't carry a pen any more, so you might need to bring a supply.

This works best when the group is seated around a table. It can be done in any restaurant, hotel or office environment, as long as the noise level allows each person to hear all the others comfortably.

Running the exercise

Distribute the torn-up paper so everyone has the same number of pieces. If you don't have time to tear the paper in advance, you can do it on the day by giving everyone a blank sheet of A4 paper and asking them to tear it into quarters as the first part of the activity.

Once each person has their blank pieces of paper (and a pen), ask them to write a question on each piece. They can be any kind of getting-to-know-you questions. Questions can be business-like, social, or as silly as you like.

To set expectations, reassure them the questions are not general knowledge such as:

> *"What's the capital of Peru?"*
> *"What's the square root of 900?"*
> *"How many bones are there in a giraffe's neck?"*

However, they can be as creative as you want. Lead by suggesting some examples:

> *"What was the best holiday you've ever been on?"*
> *"What are your goals for the coming year?"*
> *"If you were a plate of food, what would you be and why?"*

What's appropriate for one person will be completely inappropriate for another, but in a business context you probably **wouldn't** ask:

> *What's your most embarrassing experience?*
> *Which part of your body is your favourite?*
> *What's the worst disease you've ever had?*

By the way, don't mention those in advance, as it will just put the idea in people's heads. If questions like that do come up, just pitch in at that point to flag it up and explain the boundaries.

Try to discourage closed questions that have one-word answers. For example, don't ask:

"Were you a prefect at school?"

That kind of question leads to a "Yes" / "No" answer, which doesn't tell you much about the person. Remember, the objective of the exercise is to get to know each other a bit so you can build on the relationship later.

Once everyone has written their questions, ask them to fold the papers (it doesn't matter whether they fold them in halves or quarters), and put them in the hat.

Once all the questions have been submitted, shuffle them up so they are randomly distributed.

Once that's done, tell them each person is to take one question out of the hat in turn. They will read it out loud and then answer it. It doesn't matter if they draw out one of their own questions. (In fact, if they have tried to be clever with their questions and wrote something tricky, it can be most amusing when they pick it themselves.)

During the exercise

You might need to remind people to read out the question as well as their response, so the others know what they are answering.

I usually start, and then pass the hat clockwise. By going first, I set expectations for how long, detailed and even how personal the answers can be. This way, you can set the general level of levity.

If someone gives a one-word answer, it's OK to probe a bit, asking followup questions. This indicates the expected amount of detail to others. Also, it's fine to interrupt if an answer goes on for too long.

Keep going round the table until all the questions are used up, time runs out, or you've had enough. Note that, on occasions when I have had to stop this game before the end, people express their disappointment because they're enjoying themselves, and they know their own questions haven't yet been picked out for answering.

If you know time is short, it's probably better to ask people to put just one or two questions into the hat in the first place.

Some people are not comfortable sharing personal information in this way. For example, I know of someone who's very private and would consider this game a 'personal information ambush'.

Allow for this when you set up the exercise.

Give everyone the chance to raise their concerns, or say something like: "You don't have to answer any questions you don't want to. And you don't have to tell the truth. You can make up an answer – we'll never know. If you don't even want to read what's on the paper, you don't have to. You can make up a different question that you're happy to answer".

If an awkward question is read out, or a person doesn't even read it and says: "I'm not answering that", people will demand: "What's it say? What's it say?"

In this case, be ready to jump in and say immediately: "You don't have to answer that", or (shocked) "Who wrote that? Cheeky!"

Alternatively, you can deflect it saying: "Ha, ha, I know what I would say to that... but this is a business meeting / We don't know each other well enough yet / I need a few more glasses of wine first / Only my closest friends and family know the answer to that one".

After the exercise

Debrief if necessary to draw out any lessons, or use some of the answers as a starting point for a further conversation.

Variations

If time allows, it can be entertaining and informative for every person round the table to answer **every** question as it's picked out.

If you want to pre-prepare the questions instead of getting the group to write their own, here are some good ones that were adapted from playing this game with one of my mastermind groups:

- *What is your first positive memory?*
- *What was your first-ever job?*
- *What is your main memory from your schooldays?*
- *What is your favourite smell?*
- *If you could have anything, what would it be?*
- *If you could spend tomorrow any way you'd like, what would you do?*

- *What is your favourite memory of dancing?*
- *If you were King or Queen of the world, which is the first law you would change?*
- *Where do you get your best ideas?*
- *What is your favourite Sunday afternoon pastime?*
- *What did you want to be when you grew up?*
- *What memory do you return to most regularly?*
- *Where is the most distant place you have travelled?*

Comments

It turned out that one person I played this with has almost no memory, which made it impossible for him to answer any questions about his past. He remembers facts, not stories. As a result, he is thankful for the internet, immerses himself in books, and hoards things so he can look them up later. The discovery meant we could take this into account when we communicated with him afterwards.

On asking his permission to share this story, he said yes, adding: "You'll be pleased to know I have no recollection of the event at all".

Source

As far as I recall, the idea for this game came out of my own head. I've used it several times, and it always works well.

Watch the video

http://tinyurl.com/XPQuestionsInAHat

Toilet paper

Overview

This is a great energiser that works particularly well when energy dips, which might happen straight after lunch. It can also be used as a getting-to-know-you session for groups that are working together over a longer period of time such as a day or two.

Time

10-15 minutes

Number of people

10 to 1,000

In advance

All you need is toilet paper – enough rolls for the number of groups you are working with. If you haven't brought any, you might be able to borrow some rolls from the venue you're working in (and return them afterwards).

If it's a large group, first divide the audience into sub-groups of five or six people. Could be more, could be less. For a creative way to do this, please see the chapter on dividing large groups into small ones (p121).

Running the exercise

Give each group a toilet roll. This is likely to cause curiosity and laughter.

When each group has a toilet roll, tell them that each person should tear off as much or as little of the roll as they please. They will look confused, but will do as you say.

If appropriate, you can make a joke about toilet paper not being a very classy prop.

You will notice that some people tear off a tiny corner, while others reel off sheet after sheet. I sometimes comment on this, and make a joke that those people who have torn off lots of pieces might come to regret it.

When you observe that each person has some toilet paper, tell them they are to go round the group in turn, sharing fascinating facts about themselves, one for each piece they are holding.

This causes much hilarity, both for those people who've torn off a lot or a little.

During the exercise

You will notice people counting down each fact on the paper, like someone praying using rosary beads.

A person with a tiny corner of toilet paper will just say "I am a" and stop there, while a person with 25 pieces will have to share 25 separate facts.

Some groups will finish before others, but make sure that you let the exercise run to its end, otherwise people feel they are missing out. Usually, they will make conversation amongst themselves about the information that has been shared. It is unlikely that you will have to prompt them to do this.

After the exercise

As they share their corresponding facts, people often tear off each sheet, or screw up each piece of paper. As it's just paper, this is another exercise where it is pretty easy to clear up afterwards.

If time allows, you can ask for a volunteer from each group to stand and share the most interesting or hilarious fact they've learned with the whole room.

Variations

Once again, this exercise can be adapted according to your needs. For example, it can be used as a revision exercise. Instead of asking people to share fascinating facts, they can share key points they've learned so far, or any questions they may have.

Comments

As with all these activities, it's important to make the instructions clear.

One of my contacts told me she'd seen the toilet paper exercise used by a global corporate – except the facilitator forgot to tell the delegates that the number of facts they shared should correspond to the amount of toilet paper they were holding. So they obediently shared a few facts with each other, while wondering what the toilet paper had to do with it. This only made sense to my friend once she had also seen me run the exercise, and realised what the missing instruction should have been.

It is an example of how most audiences will do what you tell them, unquestioningly and without challenge. The speaker / facilitator / trainer / presenter holds a lot of power over them. That's why you – as the communicator – have a responsibility to make your instructions clear and correct.

If people are confused, they might not tell you. They will think it's their fault. Either that, or they will be too embarrassed to give you negative feedback to your face.

If someone is brave enough to tell you that you ran the exercise wrongly, or that your instructions were confusing, that's really useful to ensure you don't make the same mistake in the future.

Source

Unfortunately, I can't remember where I first experienced this exercise. However, I have used it many times in a networking or training context and it always works as a lighthearted way for people to get to know each other.

Watch the video

http://tinyurl.com/XPToiletPaper

Pennies in a basket

Overview

This is another team-building getting-to-know-you exercise and conversation starter. The game is also known as 'Never have I ever'.

The objective is to find out unexpected things about each other, share a bonding experience, have a bit of fun, and perhaps initiate followup conversations.

Time

10-20 minutes

Number of people

4 to 12

In advance

Go to the bank and get a bag of 100 pennies or equivalent small coins.

You will also need a basket. Alternatively, you can play the game using a bag, dish, bowl or other shallow receptacle.

People will need to be seated around a table in a room where the sound level allows them to hear each other clearly.

Running the exercise

Empty the pennies into the basket and place it in the centre of the table where everybody can reach.

Explain the rules of the game, as follows:

Each person in turn shares a piece of information about themselves starting with "Never have I ever..."

For example:

> *...Seen the film Rocky*
> *...Been up in a hot air balloon*
> *...Ridden a Harley Davidson motorbike*
> *...Eaten a worm*
> *...Been to Rome*

Once the person has stated the thing they've never done, anyone who **has** done that thing should take a penny out of the basket and start collecting a pile in front of them.

As with the 'Questions in the hat' exercise, I usually go first, which sets expectations for everyone else about how to proceed and gives them ideas about what kind of information to share.

During the exercise

There may be some reaction around what people say, such as teasing, incredulity, laughter, chat and banter. This it's all part of the game. It's also nice to ask people who **have** done the thing to tell everyone more about the experience.

Be cautious about how you treat the people who haven't won many – or even any – pennies, to ensure they don't feel bad. Otherwise, some people may tease them in a way that's not constructive.

When each particular topic is exhausted, play passes round the table clockwise.

You will probably go round the table at least two or three times before everyone has had enough.

At the end, the most adventurous people are rewarded because they've built up a pile of pennies in front of them. It's up to you to decide whether you allow people to keep the pennies (as their prize). Alternatively, you could ask for the pennies to be returned (although that does seem a bit mean). In my experience, people often return their pennies voluntarily.

After the exercise

Debrief as necessary to fit your theme, or continue the conversations that have arisen.

Variations

Rather than asking about adventurous experiences, you can do something that's closely related to your topic.

Penny penalties

On our Copywriting for Recruitment masterclass, I ask delegates to edit their own job ads, because they learn more by doing their own editing than they would if I did it for them.

To make this part of the day even more engaging, I give them each a pile of pennies. We then work through the list of common mistakes recruiters make. Each time they notice one of those mistakes in their own copy, they have to give up a penny (with a 5p fine for using the word 'passionate' because it's such a cliché).

It's lovely to hear the money clanging into a bowl I've placed in the centre of the table as it all comes back to me. Often, at least one person runs out of pennies and asks to borrow more.

Recruiters are generally quite competitive, and the person with the most money at the end is happy when they're announced as the winner.

It's a bit of fun – but it also symbolises the money they are leaving on the table by making those classic mistakes in their job adverts.

Source

Pennies-in-a-basket has been adapted from an exercise that was originally suggested to me by Seyi Olusanya of Cedar Events. It's used with her permission in my first tips booklet of icebreakers, published in 2005.

Watch the video

http://tinyurl.com/XPPenniesInABasket

Networking

Delegates often cite networking as the most valuable part of an event, and it can inject masses of energy into the day. Often, people come back from training courses and presentations saying that the "best bit" was the conversations they had during breaks, around the refreshment area, over lunch, or in the bar afterwards.

Good event planners allow plenty of time over lunch and refreshment breaks for people to mix, mingle and make conversation. However, it's rare for them to set the scene with an organised networking activity. Many of the icebreakers in the previous chapter can be used for that purpose. This chapter includes some more ideas.

In this section

- Networking bingo
- Say hello
- Count to 20
- Name game
- Yes and / Yes but
- The networking handshake
- Eye contact

Networking bingo

Overview

This works for any number of people, but requires a bit of preparation.

Note that people will need space to mingle without falling over chairs.

It's a great exercise to run just before a break, because it creates a real buzz in the room, and gives people lots of potential things to talk about.

Time

10-20 minutes

Number of people

10 to 100

In advance

Pre-prepare sufficient bingo sheets for the number of attendees. I usually include 20 characteristics and allow ten minutes to run the exercise. That is 30 seconds per category, and encourages fast interaction. If time is short, you can have fewer than 20 characteristics on your list (as shown below). However many you include, I suggest sticking with 30 seconds per category as that keeps the pace up.

Here's an example of a bingo sheet comprising ten categories:

1. Hates tea	
2. Is an Associate or Professional member of the PSA	
3. Lives in Glasgow	
4. Has visited another PSA region	
5. Has written a book	
6. Is a first-time guest	
7. Is active on LinkedIn	
8. First name begins with J	
9. Is wearing something blue	
10. Is a member of the PSA Scotland Facebook group	

Networking BINGO!

Find more fun ice-breakers at jackiebarrie.com

For branding, I suggest you include the event logo as well as your own logo at the top or side of the page, and add your web address as a call to action in the footer.

Suggested categories:

- *Clothing e.g. Wearing something blue*

- *Names e.g. First name starts with M*
  (This is easier if you have seen the delegate list in
  advance)
- *Behaviours e.g. Checks their email only once per day*
- *Qualifications e.g. Member of XYZ organisation*
- *Hobbies and interests e.g. Plays tennis*

Of course, you can choose categories that are directly connected with the topic you are training or speaking about. Going through them afterwards and seeing a show of hands for each one can be part of the learning.

Including some non-work categories gives people permission to extend their coffee break conversation beyond work, and creates a more relaxed and informal atmosphere throughout the day.

You might also need to provide pens.

I can guarantee that there will be a lot of noise, so take a whistle, party hooter or mini-gong – something that will be heard over the hubbub.

Also take a stopwatch or use the timer function on your smartphone.

Provide a prize. This might be a bottle of wine in a gift bag, some business books tied up in a raffia bow, or a box of chocolates.

Top tip: *If you give a bottle as a prize, I suggest you add your business card as a gift tag to help the winner remember you afterwards. Pierce a hole through your card using a hole-punch, and tie it round the neck of the bottle with ribbon. Alternatively,* *print a sticker with your business name and contact details on, and stick this over the product label. The point is to make it look like a gift from you, not from whatever brand of wine you purchased.*

If the event is free to attendees, or you are doing it as an unpaid showcase, you might not want to spend money on a prize. In this case, you can award the winner the chance to present their business to the audience for one minute. It's a priceless opportunity for them to advertise their brand, product or service in the hope of triggering followup enquiries. How well (or badly) they do is up to them, or could lead into your next learning point.

Running the exercise

You or a volunteer should distribute the bingo sheets (and pens, if required) so everyone gets one each.

Tell the audience the aim is to collect a different signature against each category. Stress that participants are not allowed to sign their own bingo sheet.

You may have to mention that they will have to get out of their seats and walk about. This sets expectations, builds excitement, and encourages them to mingle. Audiences are generally obedient and will do exactly what you say. They only need permission to get started and have fun.

It's important to tell them to wait until you say, "Go", otherwise, people will move around the room before you have completed the instructions.

Also tell them that it's against the clock. This gets their competitive spirit going, and you will probably see some people starting to shift in their seats, impatient to get started. If someone gets up before you say, "Go", you might need to jokingly address that, and gently remind them to wait. This will undoubtedly get a laugh.

Tell them that the first person to complete their sheet should shout "Bingo" at the top of their voice. If no one has completed the sheet when time is up, you will blow the whistle and the person with the most signatures by then will be the winner.

Blow your whistle to start the exercise, or just shout, "Go!"

Be sure to start your timer at this point (it's frighteningly easy to forget this in the excitement of the moment).

During the exercise

You will see people initially collecting signatures from those nearest to them. More and more people will get out of their seats and start moving around. The noise level quickly increases.

Eventually, someone will ask you if you are playing.

It's up to you, but for me, the answer is "Yes". I keep a pen in my hand ready to sign a relevant category for anyone who asks me.

Listen out for someone shouting "Bingo". When they do, you might need to blow your whistle or shout to get everyone's attention. People will probably be so immersed they will want to continue playing. It can take a while for the room to calm down and for people to return to their seats.

Alternatively, the time will run out before anyone completes their bingo sheet. In this case, you can choose whether to extend the time if that feels right. (They are unlikely to notice but you can mention it if you want to and explain that you didn't want to stop them enjoying themselves.)

If time runs out, invite everyone to go back to their seats, and then count down from 20 (or however many categories you had on your list).

> *Say: "Hands up if you have collected 20 signatures"*

> *No-one will.*

> *Say: "19?"*

> *"18?"*

> *...and so on until somebody puts up their hand.*

You might find that more than one person has collected an equal number of signatures.

In that case, you can declare a draw and the winners will have to share the prize, or you might have brought extra prizes, or you might do a tiebreaker to identify one winner.

You might need to address a sense of disappointment from the 'losers', especially anyone who had nearly finished their sheet. It's a sign of how engrossed they were in the exercise, and how much they were enjoying themselves.

Depending on who has called "Bingo", some people may shout, "Fix!". You have to be ready for anything, but I see it as all part of the fun.

After the exercise

Take the winner's bingo sheet and double-check that all the signatures they have collected look different. If not, tell the audience, send the person back to continue, and start the game again. (This has only happened to me a couple of times.)

When you eventually have a winner, give them the prize, and initiate a round of applause for them.

Top tip: If you are giving away a copy of your own book as a prize, it is a sneaky way of letting the delegates know that you are an author, without having to hard sell or promote the book.

Treat your book with respect and the audience will do the same. Stroke the book cover as you hold it up, read out the title as you explain the prize they've won, then pass the book through the audience so as many people as possible get their hands on it before it reaches the winner. This creates a small amount of jealousy. The losers want to get the book too – in fact, you might choose to bring some spare copies because some of them might be inspired to buy it.

After I've run this activity with networking groups, I ask: "But is it really networking?"

I usually get a mix of "Yes" and "No" answers.

I then go on to explain the difference between the bingo game, which I think of as 'quantity' networking (speed networking is another example), compared with 'quality' networking (which, in my view, is more likely to achieve results).

You really want to meet select people who can introduce you to the exact clients or suppliers or partners you're looking for. Usually, meeting as many people as possible in a short amount of time doesn't lead to referrals. Why would it?

If I'm doing a networking skills course, I would go on to run a separate exercise to give an example of quality networking.

For example, I first get people into groups or pairs (see the separate chapter about this, p121). I then invite them to spend time telling each other about their businesses, finding things they have in common, discovering their respective wants and needs, and ultimately making useful connections for each other (once a relationship has been built, and trust, liking and understanding have grown).

I stress that the secret of networking success is the followup – the one-to-one meetings that happen **after** the networking event. It might be a private conversation immediately afterwards, or a series of phone calls, emails or meetings in the subsequent weeks, months, or even years.

Variation 1

If time allows, you can run through the list of categories once everyone is back in their seat, and request a show of hands for each one. This can be quite fun and revealing, depending on the categories you have chosen.

For example, I sometimes put 'scuba diver' as a category. This is a hobby that the average audience wouldn't expect me to have just by looking at me, because I don't fit the stereotypical profile. When I admit it during the debrief part of the session, and the other scuba divers raise their hands, I then make the underwater symbol for OK. All we scuba divers can identify each other and chat about the underwater world during the break. You can draw a lesson from this. For example, in social media training, I stress that it's OK for business people to talk about social activities, because networking is about building relationships before growing sales.

Note that, if you include the debrief part of this exercise, it can take at least as long as the exercise itself.

Variation 2

Networking guru*, Andy Lopata, has built on my bingo idea by making it even more personalised.

He contacts participants in advance to ascertain a fascinating fact to use on the bingo sheet. It needs to be something about themselves they are happy to share, that their colleagues don't already know. It can be very revealing and stimulate some wonderful conversations afterwards.

Given that the objective of networking is to start a conversation, personalised bingo is an effective way to achieve that.

Here are some (edited) examples:

- *Has appeared on BBC news*
- *Was confronted by an angry elephant*
- *Is learning to speak Japanese*
- *Collects Smurfs*

- *Won a knobbly knees competition*
- *Competed in the World Disco Dancing Championships*
- *Has a PhD in molecular biology*
- *Danced in a West End theatre*
- *Delivered his wife's baby in a taxi*

Andy presents the criteria he's collected in a grid format on A4 landscape paper.

However you design your bingo sheet, remember to leave room for the signatures.

*He hates being called that!

Variation 3

Hand out bingo grids with room for **two** answers under each category heading e.g.

- *Shoe size*
- *Number of children*
- *Middle name*
- *Home town*
- *Favourite animal*

First, participants fill in their own answers. Then they mingle round the room trying to find a match for each of their responses. This helps people find shared interests and start conversations.

To be honest, you don't even need a bingo sheet for this; you can do it verbally. For example, I was at a networking event where Heather White got people to talk in pairs until they found something they had in common, and then shared the results with the whole group.

Comments

I have been calling this exercise 'networking bingo' since at least 2006 (that's when I first published the instructions in my first tips booklet about icebreakers).

For years, I couldn't find anyone else calling it by the same name or running it the same way. These days, you'll find references to networking bingo all over Google. There are even online tools to help create your own 'people bingo' cards, including:

- 5 x 5 bingo card maker
  teach-nology.com/web_tools/materials/bingo/5

- Print bingo
  print-bingo.com/index.php

Offline, in 2018 I was sent a 'Human bingo' card by the organisers of The Big Lunch. This is an annual event in the UK sponsored by the Eden Project and the National Lottery designed to foster community spirit by encouraging neighbours to share a lunch one weekend in June. They designed the card as a useful way to get people chatting. Here's a scan:

FIND SOMEONE WHO...

WAS BORN IN ANOTHER COUNTRY	HAS ONLY MOVED HOUSE ONCE
CAN MAKE BUNTING	CAN FIX A BIKE
KNOWS HOW TO KNIT	IS A VEGETARIAN
HAS READ A BOOK THAT YOU'VE READ	IS REALLY GOOD AT BAKING
HAS GROWN TOMATOES	HAS AN UNUSUAL TALENT

ON YOUR MARKS, GET SET, CHAT!

Source

I first experienced this icebreaker over 20 years ago when I was in corporate life. At that time it was just called bingo. We were each given a bingo card, A5 size, with a grid showing 16 different characteristics. We were asked to go round the group, collecting signatures against each one. The first person to collect four signatures in a row (up, down or diagonal) was the winner.

I amended this icebreaker for the networking groups that I used to run in the early 2000s. Rather than create any number of different bingo cards, I created a bespoke list of 20 characteristics and printed them as a table on a sheet of A4 paper, with an empty cell beside each characteristic.

Of course, your list can be tailored as appropriate for your event. It can be as serious or silly as you want.

I usually make a different list depending on the audience.

For example, for a group of accountants, I made a businesslike list with a financial bias. For an informal evening event for a network of businesswomen, the list I made was female-focused, humorous, and even a bit rude. (I haven't dared re-use that particular list since, although it was so effective that at least one attendee from that event remembered it years later, and recommended me as a result.)

Watch the video

http://tinyurl.com/XPNetworkingBingo

Say hello

Overview

This is an easy warm-up exercise that works well just before a break. The objective is for the audience to experience different styles of greeting, so they can make a better first impression and therefore improve business relationships in future.

Time

5-10 minutes

Number of people

10 to 50

In advance

You need a room where there is enough space for everyone to move about, even if that means pushing all the chairs to the sides.

No preparation is required, except for thinking of a few communication styles that might suit your audience.

You might need to take a whistle, gong, party hooter or other means of making a noise to get everyone's attention. The Mexican shush works too (be sure to practice it in advance) – it's described in the chapter about getting people into groups (p121).

Running the exercise

Tell the audience to move around the room slowly. Whenever they make eye contact with someone, they should say "Hello" in the most neutral way they possibly can. Tell them there is to be no touching – so no handshakes, hugs or kisses. Just the plain and simple word: "Hello".

Allow this to happen for up to a minute. No more. You'll sense when they've had enough.

Next, invite the audience to repeat the exercise, but this time they should say "Hello" as if they won the lottery last night. (Pick another style if that suits your audience better e.g. won a big new contract, won an Oscar, or won employee of the month.)

Set them off again and observe the difference in noise levels and enthusiasm.

Next, ask them to do it again, but this time as if they have a secret.

Again, it might be appropriate to call out the difference in energy.

Repeat with different styles as often as makes sense, but try to end with a positive one. For example, tell them to "Say hello as if you're meeting your very best friend who's just got off the plane after being away for the past five years".

This ensures the exercise ends on a joyful and happy note, but you might need to remind them of the 'no touching' rule, especially before they do this one.

During the exercise

Some people will get into this more than others. Maybe seek out the ones who look as though they're not quite as engaged, and say "Hello" nicely to them.

After the exercise

Host a quick discussion about what it feels like to be greeted in various ways. Note how your response changes when you get a warm greeting compared with a cold one. What's it like to feel really welcomed?

Most people will agree that a friendly "Hello" is by far the most pleasant. This might make them rethink how they make a first impression when they meet new people.

Variations

You can play too, if you want. If you do, be sure to keep an eye on the time, and keep the activity moving along.

Once they've got the idea, you might like to invite up to three audience members to suggest their own style of saying hello. This will depend how much time you have.

Someone is bound to suggest, "Say hello as if you fancy the other person". In a work environment, this will no doubt cause a smattering of nervous laughter. If it seems appropriate, allow this to happen. If not, collect another couple of suggestions and choose the best.

Source

I first experienced this exercise when John Cremer ran an 'introduction to improv' workshop at PSA London. It was the first thing he did, and worked to instantly relax me, as I realised, "Phew, I can do this". As you may notice, I went on to become a complete improv addict – but that's another story.

Watch the video

http://tinyurl.com/XPSayHello

Count to 20

Overview

This is really simple, and a great team-building exercise. It works to demonstrate the power of listening, which can be used in almost any personal development context. It's also a brilliant game to help build a 'no blame' culture.

I'm sure you can think of your own applications too.

Time

10 minutes

Number of people

5 to 25 or more (because you can have more than one group doing this at the same time)

In advance

No preparation is required, other than needing a big enough space so the group or groups have room to stand in a circle.

If it's a small group in a theatre-style layout, you might want to arrange their seats in a circle or semi-circle.

The game can also be played by separate groups seated at round tables.

Running the exercise

Tell the group/s they are to count from 1 to 20, one number at a time. No individual can say two numbers in a row (so one person can't quickly count "1, 2, 3, 4, 5..."). Here's the catch. If two or more people say the same number at the same time, they all have to start again from 1.

Tell the group/s that it's critically important to celebrate when it goes wrong – which it's bound to do. When it does, everyone should cheer and raise their arms.

Demonstrate this and get them to practice celebrating a mistake.

If they actually get to 20, the celebration can be even more extravagant.

Note that the participants are not allowed to employ any strategies. For example, they mustn't take it in turns, or indicate that they want to say the next number by putting up their hand or anything else.

Instead, they must listen hard and **sense** when it is 'their turn' to say a number.

To get them going, start by loudly announcing the number 1 the first time.

After that, they can start themselves off whenever they need to.

During the exercise

Watch out for all the creative ways people might try to 'cheat', and stop them!

Some people will decide not to say any numbers at all. Others will pick on one number and just say that each time. There might be long pauses, or the counting might climb really quickly.

You might like to join in with the cheers every time a mistake happens. Each time, it will probably cause some laughter.

The more competitive people are likely to sigh and groan each time they have to start again, and try even more intently. This can be most amusing to watch.

After the exercise

Draw out the learning by asking people to note their own personal strategies. For example, discuss how they felt about participating. Did they have an inner sense of their 'own number', and when they should speak? If they were loud, or quiet, does this relate to their interaction in meetings as well, perhaps?

How did they feel about 'failing'? What was it like to celebrate mistakes for a change? Did they notice that the failures were when the biggest laughs occurred? Make the point that mistakes are actually the best bit, because they are when the most learning happens. Can you make a parallel between this exercise and what happens in the organisation when someone makes a mistake?

Variations

If they get to 20 too quickly, you could get them to count up to 30 instead.

Keynote speaker and comedian, Celia Delaney, has another idea. She first asks people to count to 20 as a group. Then, when they can do that, replacing 2 with a clap, 5 with a mime, and 17 with a sound... They all end up falling about laughing because it is so hard. This helps people with working as a team as well as with focused listening, observing and paying attention.

Source

This is another improv game I discovered thanks to John Cremer. I first played it on a holistic holiday on a Greek island where he was teaching. I've also played it at a teenager's birthday party and during a family Christmas party.

Watch the video

http://tinyurl.com/XPCountTo20

Name game

Overview

With a small group of people who don't know each other, it's typical for a facilitator to go round the table asking them to introduce themselves – but that can be dull.

So here are some other creative ways to learn names. They build up to a really high-energy finish, perfect for going straight to a break.

Time

5 minutes

Number of people

10 to 50

In advance

Clear a space and ask everyone to stand in a big circle.

Running the exercise

Part 1

Tell them they are to point at someone else in the circle, make eye contact with them, and say their **own** name. You start. For example, if it's me, I'll point at someone – anyone – and say "Jackie".

You don't need to keep pointing, just drop your arm back to your side.

Whoever gets pointed at then points at someone else, and does the same thing.

This is surprisingly hard to get right, as some people will no doubt say the name of the person they are pointing at instead of saying their own name.

As with the 'Count to 20' exercise, part of the joy is in celebrating failure. So get everyone to practice cheering and raising their arms when it goes wrong.

Keep going until everyone in the circle has said their own name at least once.

With a big group, you might have to ask anyone who hasn't yet had a turn to put their hand up. Make sure they get included.

Part 2

This time, tell people to point at someone else in the circle and say that person's name. Hopefully, they will have remembered at least some of the names from the previous round.

As before, you start it off, and make sure everyone has at least one turn.

Again, celebrate any mistakes, because those are not important. It's not life or death, and the mistakes are the best and funniest bit – which is a great life lesson.

Part 3

Get people to make eye contact with someone, point at them, say "YOU!!!" and run towards them to give them a high ten (that is, slap both their hands together at shoulder height). Then it's their turn to run across the circle and high ten someone else.

This is sure to get laughter and energy in the room.

With a big group, you can start more than one 'chain' going. Once the first pattern is underway, simply start another one. Eventually, you will have lots of people running across the circle, which is a great energiser.

During the exercise

You might have to clarify the instructions once or twice, just in case not everyone listens or understands the first time. If this happens, accept that it's your fault not theirs, so apologise for not being clear.

After the exercise

If you've ended with the 'high ten' activity, people will be buzzing from running about. Lead them straight into coffee or lunch so they can continue their high-energy conversations.

Variation 1

Make a big circle. Make eye contact with someone across the circle and point at them, saying their name out loud.

When they hear their name, they nod.

You then walk across the circle to take their place as they name another person and walk across to them.

Alternatively, rather than walking one at a time, everyone can stay put with their pointing arm raised, and wait until everyone is pointing at someone else. Then ask them **all** to walk to wherever they're pointing, so everyone changes places at the same time. Chaos and laughter will no doubt ensue.

Variation 2

Get everyone into a circle. Ask them to point their right hand upwards (including you).

Drop your hand so you're pointing at someone in the circle and say your own name. Keep pointing. The person you're pointing at then points to someone else and says their own name, and so on.

You can tell if someone hasn't been included yet because their hand will still be pointing upwards. Eventually, there will be a complete criss-crossing chain of people all pointing at each other, that starts with you and comes back to you.

Repeat the exercise a couple of times non-stop in exactly the same order (getting faster each time).

Once the pattern is learned, you could repeat it without the pointing. This time, everyone says their own name in the same order, at speed. Repeat this two or three times, non-stop.

If you want to mix it up even more, get a different person to start a new pattern. Eventually, you can try both patterns together, or even get three going at once.

Ultimately, when everyone knows everyone's names, repeat the whole exercise saying the name of the person you are pointing to, instead of your own name.

Variation 3

Ask everyone to make a big circle and introduce themselves to the person on their left (if they haven't already done so). Then ask everyone to move to a new space in the room ensuring they can still see the person they were looking at.

Ask them all to close their eyes and strike a pose. They should then open their eyes and slowly morph into the pose of the person they are watching. Meanwhile, that person will be slowly morphing into the pose of someone else. It's like a lovely slow group dance.

Allow the movement to continue for a short while. The group might eventually reach consensus on a common pose, or they may not. Either way, you can draw out a lesson about groupthink or togetherness.

Play this variation a few times so people can get to know a new person each time.

Source

These ideas were inspired by some of warm-up games I experienced at the Maydays twice-yearly improv retreat in Dorset. (That's John Cremer's troupe – as previously mentioned, I've become addicted to improv, and have trained with them many times now.)

I've since used the name game for a PSA active networking session (and at a children's party), where it worked really well.

Watch the video

http://tinyurl.com/XPNameGame

Yes and / Yes but

Overview

This exercise is a simple way of showing how language impacts results.

It would make sense within a session about project planning, to improve interpersonal communications, or to help effect cultural change, for example.

It can also be used in a networking context as a novel way for people to meet others and generate potential business opportunities.

Time

10-15 minutes

Number of people

10 to 200

In advance

No preparation is required, except a little bit of thought into suitable opening lines that you can use to inspire conversation.

Ideally, it will be done standing with plenty of room for people to move about, so they can meet maximum people in minimum time. Alternatively, they can work with the person sitting beside them or behind them.

Running the exercise

Part 1

Tell the audience to pair up. If they are standing, you could divide the room into two halves. Tell one half they are As and the other half are Bs. All the As then have to find a B as their partner. Alternatively, you can make pairs by using one of the activities in the chapter about getting people into groups (p121). If there is one person left over, they can work with you.

Tell the newly formed pairs they will have a conversation, in turns, one sentence at a time. The As will go first. You will give them the opening line. The only rule is that whatever each person says next **must** start with the words "Yes, and…'

Give them a first line e.g. "Let's decorate the room".

Allow the conversations to go on for about a minute, then get their attention with a whistle, gong or Mexican shush as described in the chapter on groups (p141).

Part 2

Tell them to rearrange themselves into different pairings, still with As paired with Bs.

This time, they will have a conversation where each line starts with the words "Yes, but…"

Again, the A people go first.

Give them a new opening line e.g. "Let's go on holiday together".

Again, allow the conversations to last about a minute before calling for silence and moving to part 3.

Part 3

Repeat part 1 ("Yes, and...") in new pairings so the activity ends on a high.

This time, you could invite them to choose their own opening line, or suggest a suitable one e.g. "Let's start a joint venture".

During the exercise

In part 1, the noise level in the room will quickly increase, and there will probably be some laughter.

During "Yes and" conversations, people's imaginations will soon run away with them. For example, they might say:

> *"Yes, and we can go to the moon"*
> *"Yes, and we can make a video of our trip"*
> *"Yes, and the video might go viral"*
> *"Yes, and then we can make our fortune"*
> *"Yes, and we can retire and sit on the beach"*

In part 2, the energy level will probably be quite different as the conversations are likely to spiral downwards into negativity. For example:

> *"Yes, but I'm afraid of the sea"*
> *"Yes, but you can get hypnosis to help with that"*
> *"Yes, but I tried that before and it didn't work"*
> *"Yes, but I know a really good hypnotherapist"*
> *"Yes, but I don't really trust your recommendations"*

In part 3 (where people say "Yes, and" again), some of the conversations might turn out to be genuinely useful rather than surreal. Either way, it will end the exercise on a good note.

After the exercise

Here are some of the learning points you can draw out from this activity.

Draw people's attention to the different energy levels during "Yes, and" and "Yes, but" conversations.

You could point out that "Yes, but" really means "No".

Ask the A people how it felt when their original idea was built on by their partner. Was it satisfying? How did it compare with the "Yes, but" conversation when their original suggestion was repeatedly stomped on? With "Yes, but", how hard was it for them to stick to their proposal? Discuss if that ever happens in their workplace and what they could do about it.

Ask the B people to share how easy or difficult it was for them to have "Yes, and" or "Yes, but" conversations. Did anyone find they tended to say "Yes, but" even when they were supposed to say "Yes, and"?

Discuss how a "Yes, and" approach could improve their relationships, or how refreshing a "Yes, and" culture would be within their project team or the organisation where they work.

Source

I learned this thanks to John Cremer at my first improv workshop at PSA London, because "Yes, and" is one of the three key principles of improvisation. In an improv scene you have to accept what your partner suggests and build on it. That doesn't mean you have to like it.

For example:

> *"Here's a green dragon for you"*
> *"Yes, and it's really lovely"*
> *OR*
> *"But I'm allergic to dragons!"*
>
> *NOT*
>
> *"That's not a dragon, it's an alien"*

Watch the video

http://tinyurl.com/XPYesAndYesBut

The networking handshake

Overview

It may seem overly simple and not even worth trying, however, not many people are taught how to shake hands properly. Whenever I've done this with an audience, it's always gone down well. In fact, one young accountant was so concerned to get it right that he took me aside afterwards to double-check he'd understood correctly, and to practice his new handshake.

Time

5 minutes

Number of people

10 to 100

In advance

As with many of these activities, ideally, you need a room with space for people to move about.

Running the exercise

Get people into pairs.

First, ask them to shake hands using their fingertips only.

They will do it, and groan or say "Yuk".

Explain that kind of handshake is unpleasant, and commonly known as the 'wet fish'.

Next, ask them to shake hands by gently gripping the other person's knuckles. Remind them to be careful with this one. Otherwise, when they do it, the other person might say "Ouch".

Point out that this is also an unpleasant handshake, often called the 'bone-crusher'.

Finally, hold out one of your palms with fingers and thumb spread so they can see it clearly. Point out the web of skin between your thumb and forefinger.

Tell them the best kind of networking handshake is when the web of your hand meets the web of the other person's hand. (For total clarity, you could demonstrate by putting the webs of your two hands together.)

Watch as they try this handshake.

This time, you might see people nod and hear them say: "Ooh", "Aha", "Mmm, that's better".

After the exercise

You can host a whole discussion about how each handshake felt and move on to talk about the appropriate way to greet people.

For example, is it ever OK to meet businesspeople with a kiss or a hug? When you know them really well? What about if you're meeting them for the first time? Is it different when meeting people of the opposite sex? Has greeting etiquette changed during your lifetime?

Are there cultural differences? When I was in Canada, I found that hugging was a really common way of greeting people, even complete strangers. Even in the UK, it's getting more common. In different parts of France, is it polite to exchange one kiss on the cheek, two, or even three?

You might mention that what people really shouldn't do is tickle the other person's palm when you shake their hand. That's just creepy. And gentlemen, unless you're really theatrical, please don't kiss a lady's hand when you meet. It's not the seventeenth century.

Variations

Depending on the room layout and interactivity level of your session, you could invite a pair of people on stage to demonstrate each handshake before the rest of the audience have a go themselves. Alternatively, you could invite six people on stage to do the demo in three pairs of two.

Source

I first witnessed this activity at a networking session run at the Selsdon Park Hotel in Croydon by Caroline Hinkes.

Eye contact

Overview

Again, this may seem overly simple, but people don't know what they don't know so it may be worth trying if it fits with your objectives.

Time

5 minutes

Number of people

10 to 100

In advance

No preparation is required except for getting people into pairs.

Running the exercise

Tell people they will have to look into each other's eyes (they'll probably laugh at this point).

Tell one person in each pair to try looking in a triangle that extends to include each eyebrow and the tip of the other person's nose.

The other person should raise their hand whenever they think eye contact has been broken.

The purpose of the exercise is to demonstrate how easy it is to appear to be making eye contact even when you're not.

Some people find it very useful if they are ever in a conversation with someone they don't particularly like, because it seems to the other person that they are looking into their eyes when in fact they're not.

After the exercise

Discuss the importance of eye contact in communication.

Variation 1

Here is another activity that demonstrates the power of eye contact.

Ask the audience to get their house or car keys from their bag or pocket. (When you tell them this, they'll probably joke about putting the keys in a bowl at a partner-swapping party.) This won't work if everyone is staying in a hotel overnight, as their keys might be in their room and their hotel key card won't be a good replacement as the activity needs something weightier than that.

Standing in pairs, the first person holds their keys at waist height. The other person faces them with their hands at their side.

At a moment of their choosing, the first person should drop the keys. The other person has to try to catch the keys before they reach the floor. (It involves bending and stretching, so don't try this if your audience members have mobility problems.)

Most people will watch the hand holding the keys, and will fail to catch them as they fall. Let them try a few times. Celebrate if anyone succeeds.

Let the pairs swap over so the other person drops their keys and the first person tries to catch them.

Interestingly, this isn't (just) about speedy reactions.

Then tell them the secret tip. Instead of watching the hand holding the keys, try it while watching the person's eyes. There is something in their eyes that gives away the moment they will drop the keys before their hand actually lets go, and gives you much more chance of catching them.

Let people try this and notice the difference.

Variation 2

Similarly, there is an exercise called Dutch clapping that I learned on a Maydays improv retreat.

Standing in pairs facing each other, each person claps their own hands together, and then chooses whether to throw both hands to their left, right, up or down. They then repeat the handclap and throw again, in the same or another direction of their choice.

Each person does this simultaneously.

If both people coincidentally throw their hands in the same direction, they clap their own hands again then high ten (clap each other's hands high) before continuing.

Keep the rhythm going as long as you want.

Again, the tip here is to look into the other person's eyes rather than watching their hands.

This may be counter-intuitive, but it works.

You can use it as a fun and high-energy way of leading into a discussion about eye contact and communication, for example.

Source

I learned the eye contact activity on a corporate awayday in Guildford when I was working at Freemans home shopping in the 1980s and '90s.

Breaking large groups into small groups or pairs

During your training session or speech, you might want to divide a large group into smaller groups or pairs. Often, it's because you want them to compare notes and recall key learning points, or to discuss questions they might want to ask.

This can be particularly valuable if you are speaking in a country where English is not the attendees' first language. It gives them a chance to relax from concentrating on what you are saying, and to speak to their neighbour in their own tongue.

Most speakers or trainers will ask people to talk to the person sitting next to them, or to the people sitting in the same row or around the same table. However, many people choose to sit next to someone they already know. This means they will be having a conversation with a person who is likely to be similar to themselves. Somebody they could talk to anytime.

Meeting new people is an important part of the audience experience. So, rather than asking people to work with whoever they are sitting nearest to, it can be interesting to mix them up a bit.

Making people move about injects energy into the room. It also gets oxygen-rich blood flowing to their brains.

However, people don't like doing things for no reason. To introduce these exercises, it's best to 'call it out' by saying something like "It feels as though we've been sitting still for a long time and need to get some energy into the room".

Note that some of the activities in this section won't be suitable if you have participants with mobility issues, so you'll have to use your judgement on that.

In this section

- Fuzzy balls
- Index cards (file cards)
- Line up
- Islands
- Mexican shush
- Introverts
- In groups / Out groups

Fuzzy balls

Overview

This is a great way of dividing a big group into smaller groups. It's more original than having a coloured dot stuck on their name badge – that's been done so often that people easily second-guess what it means.

On the other hand, audience members probably haven't seen fuzzy balls used before. This means they experience a strong sense of anticipation when you give them out – which is exactly the mood you want people to be in for your session.

Time

2-5 minutes

Number of people

10 to 1,000 or more

In advance

First, you need to know how many people will be attending your event in total, and how many you want in each sub-group.

You will then need to buy enough fuzzy craft balls to make sufficient different matching sets for your sub-groups. You'll find sackloads on Amazon (search 'pom poms') as well as small bags of them in your local toy store or craft shop. They are supplied bundled into random colours and sizes. Some are sparkly.

The only downside is that sorting them out can be a bit fiddly and tedious, as you will always have more colours and sizes than you need.

Running the exercise

Tell people they will each need a fuzzy craft ball. Ensure you have a volunteer or two lined up who will help you distribute fuzzy balls to anyone that hasn't already got one. (See the Variations section below for other ways to distribute them.)

When the room has quietened down, tell them they now need to find the other people with the same size and colour of balls as their own.

I usually make a jokey apology before I say this – often, some of the people in the audience have anticipated what I'm about to say and start laughing even before I say it. I might lead into it with: "And here is something I always enjoy saying" or "And here is something you won't hear me say very often".

By the way, this mild cheekiness works perfectly well for mixed audiences as well as groups of all men or all women. By being ever so slightly unexpected and naughty, it's just inherently childish and funny.

During the exercise

People will stand up, often holding their fuzzy ball high in the air, and shouting out its colour and size.

It can be a source of much amusement to hear otherwise dignified people calling things like, "Who's got big red balls?" or "Small blue balls over here!"

Enjoy letting them make up their own jokes; people usually remain just about professional. Anyway, I've never yet had to step in and calm down the merriment.

If it's a big space, you might have to guide some people into their sub-groups if they can't find them.

If the sums don't add up, for example, there are absentees so there's not an equal number of people to fuzzy balls, you might also have to invite any 'odd' people to join another group. Make sure no-one is left out.

Once everyone is in their sub-groups, they'll probably start chatting, so blow your whistle to grab their attention (or use whichever noise-making device you've brought along).

After the exercise

Run straight into whatever sub-group activity you have planned.

You might want to collect the fuzzy balls afterwards, although people often like to keep them as a souvenir, because they're very tactile. After doing this with a group of over 50 people, I once got only two fuzzy balls back, and I know that one member of my mastermind group kept hers in her handbag for at least a year.

Variations

Obviously, you can replace the fuzzy craft balls with any other prop that has sufficient variations for the number of sub-groups you need. For example, you can get coloured feathers or pipe cleaners in craft shops and toy stores. Have a browse around; you're sure to find other items that will work just as well.

If you're handing the fuzzy balls out at registration, it might be wise to warn the organiser in advance what you're planning, so they can brief their reception team.

Ensure you get there early to give them a supply of fuzzy balls all mixed up in a bucket or other container, and check they understand what you need – that is, on arrival, that each attendee should pick one fuzzy ball of their choice and take it in with them.

When it's time to run the exercise, you will notice people rummaging around in their pocket or handbag, or on the floor, wherever they've put it.

Sometimes, I take a bowl that is large enough to hold all the fuzzy balls, and make a sign that tells people 'Please take one'. I display this on the reception desk where they sign in.

Source

I first experienced this way of forming groups at a three-day Advanced MindStore event in Glasgow, in the late 1990s. There were about 2,000 people in the room.

At registration, there was a bucket full of fuzzy craft balls, and we were each invited to take one. It felt like an intriguing and delicious choice. At a certain point in the proceedings, we had to get up and find the other people with a matching craft ball, and found ourselves in groups of ten.

The effectiveness of this technique obviously stuck in my mind, and I've often used it since.

Watch the video

http://tinyurl.com/XPFuzzyBalls

Index cards (File cards)

Overview

This is another fun way of dividing a big group into smaller ones. However, it takes a bit of thought and planning.

The objective is to mix people up in a way that gets more energy into the room than it does by simply saying: "Pair up with the person on your right" (which of course never works because everyone turns to their right), or "Work with the nearest people in your row", or "Shift your chairs into groups of five".

You'll find lots of ideas for ways to use cards in this chapter. How could you use them to help achieve your objective?

Time

About 5 minutes

Number of people

10 to 100

In advance

You will need to buy white or coloured index cards – as many as you need to give one to each attendee.

Decide how many people you want in each sub-group, and write the corresponding number of words or phrases on the cards.

You will find lots of lists to inspire you when you do some Google searching e.g. Search 'Famous pairs', 'Famous couples' or 'Groups of four'.

Example pairs:

> *Victoria and Albert*
> *Fish and Chips*
> *Gin and Tonic*
> *Cat and Mouse*

Example threes:

> *Veni, Vidi, Vici*
> *Tom, Dick, Harry*
> *Peter Pan, Wendy, Captain Hook*
> *Snap, Crackle, Pop*

Example fours:

> *North, South, East, West*
> *John, Paul, George, Ringo*
> *Spring, Summer, Autumn, Winter*
> *Clubs, Diamonds, Hearts, Spades*

Example fives:

> *Scary, Ginger, Posh, Baby, Sporty (The Spice Girls)*
> *Lion, Rhino, Elephant, Buffalo, Leopard (Africa's 'Big five')*

> *London, Paris, Washington DC, Munich, Canberra (Capital cities)*
> *Dave Dee, Dozy, Beaky, Mick, Titch (UK band from the 1960s)*

The words you choose will depend on your theme or topic and the general knowledge of your audience, so make sure you choose things that are culturally relevant.

You could even use key words, concepts or jargon from your own course materials.

Ensure the index cards are mixed up and placed on the chairs or tables in the break before your session. (They could be inside envelopes if you are using those – see the Envelopes section in the Miscellaneous chapter for details, p189.)

Running the exercise

Tell people to look at the word or phrase on their index card. Allow time for them to rummage about and find it.

Tell them they will have to get up and find the people or person with a matching word or phrase on their card.

I usually joke that once someone tried to match Julia Roberts with whipped cream – and that's not how it's supposed to work. This is a true story, and it always gets a laugh.

During the exercise

People will wander round the room shouting out their own word or phrase, and / or their guess for the word or phrase that matches it. If they hold 'Salt' for example, they'll shout out "Who's got Pepper?" or "Has anyone got Vinegar?"

Keep your eyes open for anyone who's left out because the partner to their card is absent, and discreetly invite them to join another group.

After the exercise

Once everyone has formed into their sub-groups or pairs, you'll need to quieten the room ready to run your next exercise.

Variations

One suggestion I've seen is that all the cards are pairs of animals, and that trainees have to go round the room to find their partner by making animal noises only.

At parties, it has been known for people to have a word or phrase written on a sticky note that's stuck on their forehead so they can't read it. They then have to ask "Yes / No" questions to work out their own word or phrase first, prior to finding their partner(s).

In a business context, those suggestions would only make sense if they draw out additional lessons that suit your theme.

Source

This activity was inspired by a Victorian parlour game. I'm not **that** old, but I do seem to remember my family used to play a party game similar to this when I was young.

Watch the video (Groups)

http://tinyurl.com/XPIndexCardsGroups

Watch the video (Pairs)

http://tinyurl.com/XPIndexCardsPairs

Line up

Overview

This is yet another exercise that divides a big group into smaller ones, injects energy, and mixes people up in a fun and interesting way.

Time

2-5 minutes

Number of people

10 to 100

In advance

There's no preparation required, but you do need a room that has a bit of space, whether at the back or sides of the room, or down the centre aisle.

Running the exercise

Ask people to stand up and arrange themselves in a line from one end of the room to the other.

For example, you could say that the far left side of the room is for people whose birthday is 1 January, and the far right side of the room is for people whose birthday is 31 December. Joke that you are not asking them to reveal the year of their birth.

Or you could ask them to line up alphabetically by first name, which would work as a mini getting-to-know-you session.

Or you could ask them to line up by height... or by any other criteria of your choice.

Ideally, the order you ask them to line up will depend on your objectives and topic. For example, you could get people to line up by level of experience, so you know who's an absolute beginner and who thinks they know a lot already. If you are running a session about the cultural differences between East and West, you could ask them to line up by geographical location of where they were born or where they work.

Example
I was in a musical improv session where pianist Joe Samuel asked us to line up in order of how much we wanted to be pushed and stretched compared with how much we just wanted to have fun. It enabled him and the other tutors to judge the level of challenge and support they gave us.

Case study

When I ran a couple of Q&A breakout sessions at the Pro Copywriters' conference in 2018, I asked each group to line up in alphabetical order at the start of the session. I invited them to tell everyone their name, and wrote them on a list as a creative way of taking the register.

I then asked the attendees to rearrange themselves in order of distance they'd travelled to get there. This revealed where people lived. Those from the same town were able to recognise each other and possibly arrange to meet up afterwards. It also gave me the chance to give special thanks to those who'd come a long way, especially from overseas – and to joke that the Londoners probably had a journey that took just as long.

Finally, I asked them to line up in order of how long they'd been freelancing, with newbies at one end and experts at the other. This revealed their level of experience, and helped me judge what to say and who to turn to when canvassing questions and answers. It worked really well, especially because no other breakout sessions at that event were as interactive.

During the exercise

Note that whatever category you choose is likely to create a bit of banter between the participants.

Once people have got out of their chair and chatted to people as they find their place in line, you simply go along the line grouping people into whatever you need for your next exercise.

You might walk along labelling alternate people A and B, then ask all the As to cluster together and all the Bs.

Or you might go down the line counting, "1, 2, 3, 4, 5 You're group one; 1, 2, 3, 4, 5 You're group two."

Or you could pair up people from opposite ends of the line. As with everything, it depends on the outcome you're after.

After the exercise

Once you have formed your desired sub-groups or pairs, simply lead them into your next exercise.

Variations

You can move people around the room for other purposes too.

For example, I was at an event where Caroline Hinkes had prepared coloured squares that she placed on the floor. We were invited to move to whichever colour represented our answer to each question she posed.

You don't need to bring coloured squares to do that, of course, you can just use the sides or corners of the room.

For a question that might have a more nuanced response, you can imagine the extremes at each end of the room, with answers on a continuum in between. People start by standing in the position that reflects their current thinking, and might move once you've given them additional information.

Diversity and inclusion

You might have seen the 'All that we share' video by TV2 Danmark – it has over 5 million views on YouTube at the time of writing.

Diverse people enter a big room with boxes marked on the floor. Initially, they are grouped by demographic criteria that creates a sense of 'us' and 'them'.

The people are then rearranged into categories such as:

- *Class clown*
- *Step-parent*
- *Love to dance*

It makes a strong point that we have more in common than that which divides us. Maybe you could adapt it to reinforce your own learning points? If you'd like to watch it, here's the link: youtu.be/jD8tjhVO1Tc. Warning, it's a tear-jerker!

Source

I discovered the basic 'line up' energiser at an associate day held by Kent Trainers, one of my long-term training clients.

Watch the video

http://tinyurl.com/XPLineUp

Islands

Overview

This is another exercise that gets people to move about. Remember, moving gets the blood flowing to bring oxygen to the brain, so it wakes people up and energises them.

Time

10 minutes

Number of people

20+

In advance

No preparation is required, but the room needs plenty of space to move about.

You might need to do a headcount and a bit of easy mental arithmetic.

Running the exercise

Tell the audience to form themselves into 'islands' (groups) of four. You can give them a time limit.

You could embellish the exercise by saying that they need to get onto the right island or they will be eaten by sea-monsters and die a horrible death.

(Some facilitators say sharks, but I say sea-monsters instead. As a scuba diver, I am extremely fond of sharks. I know that they don't generally eat people – at least, not deliberately – and I don't want to encourage that belief.)

When they've grouped into fours successfully, tell them to reform into groups of five. And, straight after that, groups of two, or ten.

If you are working with exactly 20 people, you will notice that the big group divides equally into all the mini-groups.

On the other hand, you might want to create groups where not everyone fits.

With a group of 20 people, you might call for groups of three. In this case, you will get 18 people successfully into mini-groups, with two leftover.

You then have to decide what to do with the 'odd ones out'.

Are they out of the game? Or do they join in with the next round?

Depending on your topic, this can lead to a discussion around what it feels like to fit in or be excluded.

During the exercise

However you introduce the activity, there will be a flurry of movement while the participants scurry about arranging themselves into groups.

You might notice some people always being slower to find the group where they can fit in, and others hugging their favourite people to them.

Those observations can also be drawn out as learning points.

Source

I first experienced this exercise during an improvisation course run by Paul Z Jackson on behalf of the Comedy Store Players. In that context, people who didn't make it onto an island had to fall to the floor and 'die', with cheers and applause for the most elaborate acting.

Watch the video

http://tinyurl.com/XPIslands

Mexican shush

Overview

Once people get chatting, you will need some way of attracting their attention. In a noisy room, you could use a whistle, party hooter or gong, but that just adds to the hubbub. Here's a quieter option (also known as the Magic shush).

Time

Less than 30 seconds

Number of people

Unlimited

In advance

Tell people when they hear you or anyone else make a "shushing" noise, they must say "shush" themselves and immediately fall silent.

So that the audience gets used to it, test it a couple of times, getting faster each time.

Running the exercise

When everyone is talking, just say "Shush" to someone near you. They should "shush" the people near them and then fall silent, so a ripple of silence passes through the room.

If it's a big group, you might choose to "shush" more than one person to instigate several ripples.

After the exercise

As soon as everyone falls silent, you can move on to the next part of your session.

Variation

Establish the convention of silence when you hold your hand in the air.

With this method, you tell the audience that if they ever see you or anyone else with their hand in the air, they must also put their own hand in the air and immediately fall silent. Practice it a couple of times, making a joke about how fast or slow they are to react. Usually, even a big roomful of noisy people will become silent in just a few seconds.

Source

The 'Mexican shush' is inspired by the so-called Mexican wave (it's called the stadium wave in North America). You might have seen this at large sports events. A number of audience members whoop while rising from their seats with their arms in the air before sitting down again, then the people beside them do the same, and so on, as the 'wave' ripples round the stadium.

I'm pretty sure the Mexican shush came from another improv retreat I attended. However, I can't remember where I first experienced the 'hands up' option.

Watch the video

https://tinyurl.com/XPMexicanShush

Thoughts on individuals and groups

Before we move on, here are some stories and ideas that address the psychology of individuals and groups.

Introverts

People who identify as introverted can find it easier to be engaged when you first ask them to think on their own, then work in pairs, then as part of a bigger group, and finally to share with the whole room.

Andy Lopata runs an exercise this way in his session 'Three steps to referral heaven'. First, he asks people to come up with their own definitions of a tip, a lead, a recommendation and a referral. Then he gets them to compare their ideas in a mini-group of three or four people, then in groups of seven or eight. Finally, he unveils his own definitions, which are:

- **Tip** = Piece of information e.g. A new company is opening in your sector
- **Lead** = Name and contact details e.g. You need to contact Bob on 123 4567 8910
- **Recommendation** = I've told Clare about you. Please mention my name when you get in touch
- **Referral** = Fiona is the CEO. She knows about you and is expecting your call

Because people have done their own thinking, they are more likely to understand the different levels than if he simply gave them the definitions on a slide or handout.

In-groups / Out-groups

When I did my psychology degree, I learned about a 1954 experiment that would be considered unethical today.

22 x 12-year-old boys were divided into two camps. Initially, the camps were kept separate from each other and given collaborative tasks to do. After a few days, each group had formed a strong identity.

In phase two, the groups had to compete against each other, which resulted in a sense of friction between them, shown by name-calling and disrespectful behaviour.

Phase three was an attempt to reconcile the two groups through shared activities – but the level of antagonism was already so great that it didn't work.

The only thing that overcame their differences and combined the groups was a shared challenge. For example, they were told they had run out of drinking water and had to work together to resolve the problem.

Maybe you could adapt the experiment by setting your different groups collaborative tasks, then competitive tasks, then an overarching shared challenge to bring them back together?

You might also be interested to watch the 'Brown eyes and blue eyes racism experiment' on YouTube. Teacher Jane Elliott ran it with 3rd graders following the assassination of Reverend Dr Martin Luther King Jr. Here's the link: youtu.be/KHxFuO2Nk-0.

Enlivening 'boring' information

When I worked at Freemans home shopping, I was asked to design a PowerPoint presentation. My memory may be faulty, but I think it was about IT.

Anyway, my in-house client told me: "My presentation is so boring that I want you to put a picture of a lingerie model in the middle, just to wake everybody up."

I refused, and said: "Why don't you re-write it so it's not boring?"

Sadly, he didn't agree. I'm not sure he even understood the point I was making. Instead, he persuaded my (male) boss to produce the slides for him.

Even when the information you want to communicate could be perceived as 'boring', there is **always** a more interesting way to present it.

For example, if you have to present weekly management figures to your team, you can present the same information using different formats such as numbers, words and visuals. Some people will be quite happy interpreting a list or table of numbers, some would prefer to read the explanatory text, and others will grasp your message best by looking at a graph, chart or infographic.

In this section

- Pub quiz
- Higher lower
- Visual flipcharts

Pub quiz

Overview

The pub quiz idea works well for various reasons. When you give out information that might otherwise be perceived as dull, people sit and passively receive it. They may well start day-dreaming and you'll never know. If you're lucky, they'll ask you questions. With a quiz, people have to actively engage their brains. This means the information you're trying to communicate is more likely to 'stick'.

Also, by mixing people into random groups, you quickly create team bonds that wouldn't otherwise exist.

The randomly created teams will usually include a diverse mix of ages, experience and knowledge, so each team has an equal chance of winning.

Because it is a team exercise, no individual is publicly embarrassed by not knowing the answer to any question. It also taps into the competitive spirit that many people have.

It's fascinating to see people's eager faces as you give out the answers. They experience the satisfaction of being right, and the pleasure of potentially winning.

Time

Up to one hour as part of a longer session, or you could dedicate a whole evening to the quiz. In that case, you'd build in time for refreshments and comfort breaks.

Number of people

Any number, divided into groups of 4 to 8

In advance

Ensure the event organiser is happy for chairs to be moved into sub-groups when you run this session, and allow time for the room to be rearranged afterwards if necessary.

You can make your quiz as easy or hard as you please.

Prepare a series of questions, possibly with multiple-choice answers. As I keep stressing, you want to ask questions that are relevant to your message.

Note that recall is different from recognition. It is harder to dredge an answer from your memory than it is to recognise the answer when you see it. Multiple-choice gives everyone a chance, because – if they don't know the answer – they can always guess.

To add extra humour in a multiple-choice quiz, one of your options can be a comedy answer.

For example, one I've used at the Professional Speaking Association that always gets a laugh is:

> Q. *"What is the PSA Foundation for?*
> *(a) To support members in financial difficulty*
> *(b) To provide training for members*
> *(c) To support bewildered Regional Presidents*

Note that, in multiple-choice tests, people tend to answer either the first or last option. This depends whether an individual is a 'primacy' or 'recency' person. Primacy people are most likely to choose the first thing they see, while recency people tend to select the last option. (Source: Graham Jones, internet psychologist)

Print out numbered pages for teams to write their answers, or provide them with sufficient blank paper.

You may also need to provide pens, because people don't always carry them these days.

Depending on the size of the room and the level of background noise, you may need a microphone and amplifier so you can be heard clearly. Please use a good one. It's so frustrating to be in a quiz team and be unable to hear the questions properly.

You will definitely need a decent sound system if your quiz has a music round. If it does, remember you or the venue will need a music performance licence.

You might hand out a picture round. To make it easier, you can provide the list of names to be matched to the pictures. Use something relevant to your topic.

For a general knowledge quiz, I've used:

- *Famous bridges*
- *Famous towers*
- *Religious symbolism*

You may need to co-opt one or two people to help you keep score.

To display the scores, you might want to pre-prepare a flipchart or whiteboard, or even project a spreadsheet onto a big screen.

Remember to buy a prize that can be shared between the number of people in the winning team.

Finally, think of a tiebreaker question in case there is a draw.

Running the exercise

Break the main group into quiz teams (possibly using the ideas in the previous chapter, p121), moving any furniture around if necessary.

Hand out answer sheets (and pens if required).

Ask each team to pick a name. One of my favourites from the home shopping world was the team who called themselves 'Pack of Five Pants'.

Choosing a team name can generate much debate, cause tension and take too much time. So, if you want to speed things along – you can allocate names to the teams. For example, if you have used the 'fuzzy balls' idea to form the teams (p123), tell them their team name is the size and colour of their fuzzy balls, such as Big Orange. Some of them will feel relaxed and relieved that you have taken this responsibility away from them and that they can get stuck into the quiz quickly.

Tell the teams how the quiz will work, including how many rounds there will be.

Explain any quiz rules, such as:

- *Mobile phones, tablets and laptops to be turned off (no Googling)*
- *The Quiz Master is always correct, even if they're wrong*

At this stage, there's usually a buzz in the room, so you'll need to quieten them down. This will happen when you say, loudly, "Question 1".

During the exercise

Ask each question clearly. Practice any tricky pronunciations in advance, and / or spell out any unusual words.

It's fair and reasonable to ask each question twice. Some teams will ask you to repeat a question a third time (or more) – this can be really annoying to pro-quizzers who will usually have written the question down or already answered it.

You want people to have a good experience, so it's important to keep things moving along quickly. That means avoiding excessive delays between rounds and during the scoring process.

After the exercise

One way of scoring is for each team to mark their own answer sheet – but that risks cheating.

It's common for nearby teams to swap answer sheets and mark each other's. This is slightly harder to manage and you may need to field questions about how many points to give e.g. If the question was to name someone and the answer only includes their first or last name, is that two points, one point or half a point?

Another way of scoring is to collect the answer sheets and mark them yourself. Better still, get a helper or two to do so. This can be the quickest and most professional approach, because you can immediately get on with asking the next round of questions.

Whatever scoring method you use, be clear, and be consistent.

When it's over, announce the scores and award the prizes.

Variations

In a quiz I ran for a membership organisation, the picture round was made up of profile photos showing all the guest speakers who'd visited in the past year. This worked to reinforce the quality of learning that regular attendees had enjoyed, as well as raising the profile of those speakers by reminding the teams about them.

For a quiz I ran when I was in corporate life, teams had to identify photos of the senior managers as children. Not many identified the picture of me as a four-year-old. When I revealed the answers, a chap from HR said, "But that's a little Indian girl!" I didn't realise my Anglo-Indian heritage showed through so much in that old black-and-white photo. (Yes, that's how old I am. Colour photography wasn't common when I was four.) The colleague – a white man – went on to complain, "But you look like one of us!" I doubt anyone would dare say something like that these days.

Also when I was in corporate life, I was asked to coordinate a conference for 200 senior managers. One of the sessions was a quiz inspired by the TV show 'Who Wants to be a Millionaire', with questions and answers based around the company information we needed to share at the event. If you ever do something like this, beware of format licensing issues, especially if the event is being recorded or broadcast.

This concept takes the quiz idea to another level, but it really worked, and was a brilliant way of communicating company facts that could otherwise have seemed dull and dry.

Comments

In one quiz I attended, the quizmaster gave double points for a multiple-choice question "because it's harder." No it isn't. An open question is harder because you need to choose your answer from a myriad of possibilities. With multiple-choice, you just have to pick one of the options you're given. However, because the quiz master is always correct (even if they're wrong), there was no point in complaining. And it evened out anyway, because every team was following the same scoring protocol.

Remember, it's supposed to be fun, so don't agonise about it.

Source

In common with any membership organisation, each regional meeting of the Professional Speaking Association (PSA) is likely to include a combination of members and guests. One of the objectives of the meetings is to persuade guests to join.

Some regions will invite guests to huddle in a corner during the coffee break so they can discover the benefits and costs of membership and have their questions answered. Other regions will present a standard message from the stage at every meeting.

The trouble is that this session is irrelevant for existing members so they don't pay attention (and this attitude spreads through the whole audience). It can also be difficult to make this 'selling' part of the event come across in an inspiring and compelling way – especially because it will probably be delivered by a volunteer who has no real financial or other incentive to recruit new members.

I know this for a fact, because I used to do it myself.

I wasn't completely unsuccessful – there are plenty of benefits to joining the PSA, and guests were only at the meeting because they were already interested. In fact, I was able to inspire many people to join. But I sensed there could be a better way. And that's when I came up with the pub quiz idea.

I've used it since in several regions and it always works really well. It's amazing to see all the enthusiastic faces turned towards you when you give out the answers, when otherwise people probably wouldn't even be listening.

Watch the video

http://tinyurl.com/XPPubQuiz

Higher / lower

Overview

You can use the higher / lower game when sharing any kind of numbers. Playing a guessing game with the audience is infinitely more interesting and engaging for them than passively presenting them with a list, table or spreadsheet.

Time

5-10 minutes

Number of people

10 to 1,000

In advance

Prepare your visual aids. Let's say you are trying to share company results from five departments. Print out five big clear visuals onto separate large-format cards, showing the relevant numbers for each department. You might want to add your branding on the backs of the cards and / or the names of the departments.

Running the exercise

Invite five volunteers to come up on stage and stand in a row facing the audience. Each volunteer represents one department. Give them your cards to hold, initially with the reverse side to the audience (that's the blank or branded side).

Ask the first volunteer to reveal their result by turning their card around. Deal with any reaction that arises, then ask the audience to guess what's on the next card by shouting "higher" or "lower", and / or waving their arms up for higher and down for lower.

Make a quick assessment of the majority decision, and repeat the higher / lower question as your volunteers reveal the other results in turn.

Keep it moving quickly, keep the banter going, and keep the energy high. For example, cheer whenever they guess an answer right, and express your own amazement if any result is particularly surprising.

During the exercise

You may need to stand to the side or in front of the volunteers as you move along the row. If you stand behind them, you can't see the answers easily so you can't respond in the moment.

After the exercise

Gather your cards, thank your volunteers, and lead the applause as they return to their seats.

Source

This game was inspired by the TV show *Play Your Cards Right*, hosted by the late Sir Bruce Forsyth.

Case study

I used to write emails inviting people to attend the Southeast regional meetings for the PSA. It turned out that we had a greater response than other regions, and head office asked me to advise other regional presidents what we'd done that was different.

I decided to share the open and click rates from a series of 50 emails we'd sent. I could have produced a spreadsheet – but the higher / lower guessing game was a better idea.

Here's how it went.

Open rates

Open rates are determined by the subject line, so I prepared a flipchart with our top ten and bottom ten subject lines mixed up. As far as I remember, they were written in alternating black and blue pen to make the headings easier to distinguish (not to separate top and bottom subject lines).

I asked the audience if they could guess whether each subject line was in the top or bottom ten. I marked their responses on the flipchart, tore off the page, and Blu Tacked it to the wall.

This revealed a second flipchart that I'd pre-prepared with the subject lines repeated in the same mixed-up order – but this time with the top ten written in green and the bottom ten in red. I'm not sure, but I might have numbered them one to ten and 40 to 50.

We then discussed what the top ten had in common. Here they are, in case you're interested:

> *PSA SE feedback (email 1)*
> *What on earth happened at our March event?*
> *You are invited to our summer party*
> *PSA South East (email 2)*
> *Fancy an informal BBQ in the Kent countryside?*
> *HAPPY BIRTHDAY TO US!*
> *Wondering who won?*
> *What happened at PSE South East March event?*
> *Are you free for dinner tonight?*
> *What are you doing on 19 May?*

It turned out that many of the top ten were a question, a 'first', or they used or implied the word 'you'. This guided the other regional presidents how to write effective subject lines in future.

Click rates

I printed out screenshots of the top ten and bottom ten emails by click rate and stuck them on pieces of A4 card. I wrote each click percentage on a Post-it note and stuck it on the back of each piece of card. The top ten were written in green pen, and the bottom ten in red pen.

I shuffled the pages to mix them up and showed the first one to the audience, asking them to guess the click rate. With no information to go on, this is not an easy task, so I quickly revealed the answer by moving the Post-it note from the back of the card to the front.

I'd briefed my co-president, Barnaby Wynter, to help with this exercise, asking him to stick all the cards with a green percentage in the top row and all the cards with a red percentage in the bottom row. I had pre-prepared each card to have a piece of Blu Tack in each corner on the back, which made it easy from him to stick the cards on the wall quickly.

Then the game really started.

I showed the audience the second email and asked them to guess if the click rate was higher or lower than the first email.

After allowing a moment for them to shout out their guesses, I revealed the answer by moving the Post-it note from back to front, and gave the card to Barnaby to add to the wall display.

Because one of the emails featured an image of Barnaby, and another featured me, it got a laugh when I asked whether his or mine got more clicks. (In case you're wondering, it was mine!)

We quickly ran through all the emails until there were two rows of ten emails sticking on the wall. High click rates on the top row, and low click rates on the bottom row.

At a glance, it was easy to see what the emails with the highest click rates had in common. In short, they each had a video image with a 'play' button, and / or a call-to-action button with an arrow and a handwritten graphic encouraging people to click.

What was most noticeable was the level of engagement of the audience. They were really keen to see the results. Some took photos of the wall display. And they all left inspired to send more creative emails. Finally, as a result of my presentation, the call-to-action graphic was changed for all emails from all regions.

Watch the video

http://tinyurl.com/XPHigherLower

Visual flipcharts

Trainers commonly use a flipchart as well as, or instead of, slides. They're great, because they are somehow more immediate. They are bespoke to that group of people, at that moment. They are co-created while the audience watch. Because they are hand-made, they seem to have a special magic that transcends slides – even if slides look more professional.

If you've asked your trainees a question, you might capture their answers on the flipchart. For example, you might start by capturing their objectives for the day so you can ensure they're covered, and refer back to them at the end as a summary.

However, there are more compelling and imaginative ways to use flipcharts. Here are some stories and tips that might inspire you.

Make them visual

On an associate day I went on with Kent Trainers, one of the other associates shared the secrets of making your flipcharts more visual.

First, draw a black outline round each page. It's amazing what a difference this makes. Most flipchart paper is white, on a white easel, maybe positioned against a white-painted wall. Drawing an outline on the pages draws the trainees' eyes to your content and makes it stand out.

Top tip*: It's easier to draw a straight line around the page when you focus your eyes in the middle of the line and use your peripheral vision, rather than trying to follow the pen with your gaze. Also, draw a deliberate squiggle or zigzag or double slashes in the middle of the lines. This means people are less likely to notice if your entire line isn't completely straight.*

When you add a heading to the flipchart page, you can enhance the text with various graphics:

- Draw a rectangular box around it. Add a drop shadow so it looks 3D
- Make it look like a scroll by drawing a curved frame with dropped ribbons at the sides
- Make it look like a flag by adding a post at the side
- Draw a cloud bubble around it
- Draw a squiggle underneath it

Boxed heading

Scroll heading

Flag heading

Cloud heading

Squiggle heading

Top down v bottom up

Although I'm a wordsmith, I'm quite visual (you might have noticed). Some of your audience will be too. By combining words with pictures and numbers, you have most chance of reaching most people.

One of my most frequent flipchart drawings uses stick-people with speech bubbles and thought bubbles. My aim is to explain that people tend to write 'I', 'us', 'we' and 'our' when talking about their business to their customers. I call this top-down language.

They want to get their message into their reader's head. But their reader already has a thought in their head: "What's in it for me?" And the only two words that answer that question are 'you' and 'your'. I call this bottom-up language.

Replacing top-down with bottom-up language is one of the ways to turn normal writing into copywriting. And when I explain it using my diagram, trainees understand it, at a glance.

Sometimes, I prepare my flipchart pages in advance and talk it through on the day. When there's more time, I draw the diagram 'live' as I commentate. I customise the graphics according to the audience. So, when I talk to landlords, I draw a house, not a person, as I say: "This is you".

If you want to draw something more interesting than a stick-person, you can draw a squiggle-person instead. It's gender stereotyping, but to draw a woman, it's a squiggle triangle with the point at the top, and to draw a man, it's a squiggle triangle with the point at the bottom. In each case, you add a circle for a head, two straight lines for arms, and two straight lines for legs.

People are impressed when you reveal beautifully designed flipchart pages that you've prepared in advance. Bring your ready-made roll of flip paper and hook it onto the easel provided by the venue. Or get there early and prepare your flipcharts on the spot, before the delegates arrive.

It's nice to start with a welcome page so people know they're in the right room as soon as they walk in. I usually write the course title, my name, the agenda times (because people always want to know when the breaks are and what time it ends), and the wifi username and password.

Flip tips

You have to treat your flipchart with respect if you want your audience to respect what you write on it. This is a tip from Celia Delaney. She noticed that some speakers (often men) fold the used flipchart page over in a careless way, leaving it crumpled at the top of the easel.

She also points out that if the legs of the easel are uneven, it will leave your audience feeling discomforted. This is due to Gestalt psychology. We are compelled to seek balance, so a wonky flipchart leg is distracting – and you don't want to distract people from your message.

On the subject of distracting your audience, I fell into a terrible trap when speaking in Cape Town. We'd all been given a goody bag that included a mini South African flag on a stand. It came in two parts – a base, and the flag itself. I noticed it at the last minute when setting up my table for my talk, and the thought crossed my mind: "Wouldn't it be nice to put the flag on the table". So I quickly stuck the parts together and got on with my presentation.

At the end, one audience member came up to me and said: "Your talk was great, but I was really distracted by the flag all the way through, because it's upsidedown." Gah! It achieved exactly the opposite effect to the one I was after. Rather than showing my respect for the country I was speaking in, I'd inadvertently insulted them. My advice is to never work with flags. They are a recipe for disaster.

Celia's final tip is to stroke the flipchart. By showing that you treasure it, the audience is more likely to treasure the message that is on it. This advice she learned as an actress when dealing with props on stage and a director told her: "The way you touch things tells people how you feel about them".

Not all perforations tear easily. The easiest way to remove flipchart pages is when you have already ripped the first couple of centimetres. (That tip is courtesy of Alan Stevens.)

To do a really neat drawing on a flipchart, pre-prepare it with pencil lines in your home office. Then you can go over them with flipchart pens on the day, and really impress your audience. (That tip is thanks to Phillip Khan Panni.)

If you want to jump to a certain flipchart page, fold the lower corner over. That way, you can find it quickly and go straight to it without ruffling all the other pages. (I don't know where I first discovered that, but I do it all the time.)

The pens provided in venues are often well used and therefore running out of ink. What's more, they might be pale green or orange – colours that can't be seen at the back. That's why a professional speaker / trainer will always take their own pens and buy new ones every three months or so. If you're working with a big audience, you'll need pens with an extra-thick nib. I always use chisel-tip pens as you get a thicker line than with bullet tips. I also have an extra-thick wedge pen called the BigOne® which I ordered online from Neuland.

Nine dots

There are certain flipchart visuals that I've drawn time and time again. One of them is the famous nine dots exercise – the origin of the expression 'to think outside the box'.

Give the audience a sheet of blank paper each and ask them to draw three parallel rows of three dots, then to go through each dot once and once only, in four straight lines, without taking their pen off the paper. Repeat the instructions so they are clear.

Most people will try to solve the problem within the invisible box containing the dots.

The answer is to draw lines that extend beyond the box. There was no instruction that you had to stay within it, but people will tend to try that because of our friend Gestalt psychology, which posits that the human brain will 'fill in the gaps' to create a box where one doesn't exist.

You can solve the problem in three straight lines by playing with the size of the dots (very small with a big pen, or very big with a small pen).

You can do it in two straight lines when you change the line into the words 'twostraightlines' written across the three rows without taking your pen off the paper.

And you can do it in one straight line by playing with the only element that hasn't been used yet – the paper. By folding or tearing the paper, you can align the dots in a single row and draw one line through them all.

Search Google for '9 dots exercise' and you'll find lots of other solutions.

I use this exercise to talk about lateral thinking and to inspire creativity. Also, to explain why copywriting doesn't have to include every single word about every single feature, because the human brain will fill in the gaps.

Uluru v Everest

On a course run by Elsevier in the 1980s, I heard a compelling story that I've remembered ever since, thanks to the flipchart visuals that accompanied it.

The speaker said: "Imagine you book a hotel with a view of Mount Everest. Fling open the windows. What do you see?"

People typically answer: "It's night-time, it's cloudy, it's snowing, it's foggy, it's a car park, it's a brick wall..."

The speaker said: "No, it's something like this". And he drew a series of triangular peaks at the top of the flipchart page, saying: "Mount Everest is in the Himalayas. It's a mountain range. And you don't know if it's this one which is nearer so it looks bigger, or that one which is further away so it looks smaller".

He continued: "Then you get the chance to visit Ayers Rock, or Uluru, in Australia. What do you see?"

People respond: "Ayers Rock".

He drew a long horizontal line at the bottom of the flipchart page, and added a tiny arc in the middle. (People laugh at this point, because they are expecting the whole horizontal line to be incorporated in the drawing.)

He explained the metaphor: "Uluru is a dirty great red rock sticking out of a flat red desert. It's much smaller than Everest, but it makes a much bigger impact. You might be the biggest and best in the world, but if you present yourself to the world the same way your competitors do, no one will notice. In your marketing, you want to be Uluru not Everest".

Metaphors like this are a really quick and effective way of communicating otherwise dry theory into people's brains. I haven't yet found a better way of explaining why brands need to be brave and be different to stand out.

Red dots

The final example is from a networking breakfast I attended in the early 2000s.

On your flipchart, draw eight dots in red, eight squares in blue, and eight triangles in green. (The quantities, colours and symbols you choose can vary.) You need to do this ahead of the course so people don't see them. Also, you need to do it on any page other than the top one, because you'll need to hide the symbols with another page.

Tell your trainees you will show them the flipchart page for three seconds, and they have to count how many red dots they see. Reveal the page… count three seconds… and cover the page again.

Then ask them how many green triangles there were. They will sigh, groan at what they see as a trick question, and a few of them will suggest some numbers. They are unlikely to be right.

Put them out of their misery and ask how many red dots they saw. They will confidently state eight.

Then reveal the page explaining there are eight of each.

With a small group, you can draw the symbols on an A4 page which you laminate or protect in a plastic wallet. With a big group, you can display the symbols on a slide.

I use this as an alternative to the famous 'selective attention test' video that many people have already seen – here's the link youtu.be/vJG698U2Mvo.

You can use it to demonstrate key points such as witnesses being unreliable, that our brains suffer from overload so we filter out anything irrelevant (which is why marketing has to be laser-focused), or that people are generally obedient.

Watch the video

http://tinyurl.com/XPVisualFlipcharts

Audience voting

As a speaker, trainer or presenter, you often want to capture audience feedback about something.

Rather than asking people to put their hands up, which is what almost everyone else does, there are some creative alternatives.

If you want to go high-tech, there is a growing choice of apps you can use to capture audience votes, while voting keypads are now used a lot, especially in US universities. With some of them, the results can be displayed in real time in the big screen.

Here are some examples at the time of writing:

- polleverywhere.com
- voxvote.com
- sli.do

To use any of these, you may need to allow time for the audience to download the relevant app to their smartphone first. You will also need to ensure the venue has good wifi and that the audience members know the password.

As you might have noticed by now, I prefer using low-tech solutions where possible. This chapter contains some ideas.

In this section

- Stand up
- Red / green

Stand up

Overview

Hands-up is too predictable, so I started using 'stand up' instead. (Note that it might not be considerate to use it if there is a wheelchair-user in the room.)

It works best when you have a series of questions, not just one, and is a very adaptable exercise. How could you use this idea to enhance your content and energise your audience?

Time

2 minutes

Number of people

10 to 1,000 or more

In advance

No preparation is required.

Running the exercise

It's really simple. Ask people to stand up if they agree with a certain statement or question you make.

Ask them to stay standing as you refine the statement or question.

At each stage, more and more people sit down.

Your goal is to end up with just one or two people standing. You can reward them with a prize.

After the exercise

Remember to tell the people who are still standing that they can sit down when you have finished with your questioning.

Variations

Stand up / stay standing can be used in all sorts of situations.

For example, Jon Baker at PSA London used it to see how many people were staying on after the meeting to go for a quick drink, and then how many were planning to go for a meal after the pub. Having people standing was a lot easier for him to do a headcount and book a table then it would have been with a show of hands, because people never raise their hand very high or clearly, or keep it in the air for long enough.

In her talk about diversity (or lack of it), Rebecca Jones asks things like "Stand up if you have pets... sit down if it's your first pet" and repeats it with topics such as "live in a flat", "have a degree" etc. If the group seems to be up for fun, she does it faster and faster with more and more silly questions. Her aim is to show people how diverse the group is because everyone is an individual.

Dr Emma Sutton uses 'stand up' as a post-break jack-in-the-box quiz to see if people can remember her core content. She says the key to success is making it fast because that creates a good buzz and laughter. She also points out that, if your speech is being translated, you'll need to ensure your questions are simple.

Example 1

I ask people to stand up if – for example – they have experienced what I consider to be the world's worst icebreaker. That is when you are asked to massage the shoulders of the person beside you, and then let them do it to you. A physical touch (without permission) has never been appropriate, isn't appropriate today, and never will be appropriate. You don't know what people have been through, and you don't know what reaction this simple request might trigger.

Usually, more than half the audience stands up, because the massage icebreaker seems to be exceedingly common, sadly.

I then say: "Sit down if you hate it". At this point, I've found that at least two-thirds of the standing people sit down.

It is patently obvious to the entire audience that the majority of the people who have experienced this icebreaker hated it. (Yes, I know hate is a strong word, but it does seem to work in this situation.)

Why would you put your audience through something that so many of them are going to hate?

I usually make a joke that the people who stayed standing because they don't mind the massage icebreaker can all go into the corner later and touch each other if they want.

Example 2

Another time I have used stand up / stay standing is in a networking context, to demonstrate the theory of six degrees of separation.

Depending on who is in the room, I will say: "Please stand up if you knew me before today". Obviously, this only works if there is at least one person you can be sure will recognise you.

I then say: "Now stand up if you know anybody who is standing". Unless the individual who knows you knows no-one else (luckily this has never happened when I've tried this exercise), a few more people will stand.

Repeat the instruction: "Stand up if you know someone who is now standing" until no-one else stands up. This will probably take four to six times.

It's a great visual example of how we are all connected through a network or series of links.

Example 3

I start a talk about websites with: "Stand up if you have a website". Almost everyone stands.

I say: "Stay standing if you have some kind of web stats or analytics on your website." A few people might sit.

I then say: "Stay standing if you've ever looked at those analytics." Usually, a whole load of people sit down at this point, and everyone laughs.

I continue by saying: "Stay standing if you have made a change to your website as a result of what the analytics tell you."

Another bunch of people sits down.

I then ask: "In the past year... six months... three months... two weeks... 24 hours..." until only one or two people remain standing. The winner(s) gets a prize and a round of applause from the audience.

It's a great way to capture attention at the start of the talk, and makes a strong point that's connected with my content.

Example 4

I've used it when asking for volunteers to participate in a live case study on stage. For example, I do a talk about taglines, and occasionally offer to attempt a 'live' rewrite for up to three volunteers.

I ask people to stand up if they are a member of a networking organisation that makes them give a one-minute pitch, or if they have a tagline or strapline they use in their marketing. Most people do.

I ask them to stay standing if they think their tagline has room for improvement. A few sit down.

Then, I ask them to stay standing if they are willing to be featured as a volunteer (this is the moment when many people sit down and everyone laughs).

Once about six people remain standing, I ask each of them to share their taglines, write them down, and then choose my volunteer(s).

Standing ovation

If you have started your talk with 'Stand up, stay standing', you've set a precedent that means you can contrive a standing ovation at the end. Just finish your talk with another question, such as 'Finally, please stand up if you've learned something useful during this session'.

With luck, plenty of people will stand and start applauding.

It's an instant measure that shows whether your message has landed. It's also a great photo opportunity for your marketing. And it's very gratifying.

Somehow, contriving a standing ovation this way is not quite as 'sneaky' as those speakers who ask the audience to stand up at the end of their talk, to put one arm out in front, then the other, then to bring both hands together with increasing rapidity. Sadly, I've seen too many speakers do this trick to think it's clever or funny.

Heads or tails

This is quite a common activity, especially at charity fundraisers. I first experienced it at a quiz in Bromley.

Ask everyone to stand up and put both hands on either their head or their tail (bottom). Toss a coin. If it lands head-side-up, people with their hands on their heads stay standing, while everyone with their hands on their tail sits down (and vice versa if the coin lands tail-side-up). Repeat until there is only one person standing. Give that person a prize.

This technique can also be used for getting a corporate message across, suggests Barnaby Wynter. He asks people to put their hands on their head if they think it's a true statement, hands on their bottom if they think it's false. Within 20 questions, it's usually down to last few people. For added drama, he brings the last five people up onto the stage for the final few questions.

Source

My version of stand up / stay standing was partly inspired by Graham Norton's 'So' TV show from a few years ago, and partly thanks to an e-conversation I had with an American speaker called Bill that happened on Ecademy, the online business network that's now offline so I can't track him down.

Watch the video

1:47

http://tinyurl.com/XPStandUp

Red / green

Overview

Speakers often want a quick and easy way to know what your audience thinks about your content. But asking for a show of hands is boring. Public voting using a colourful prop creates a highly visual flutter of energy as people participate 'live' in your talk. (By contrast, David Gouthro sometimes likes people to be more subtle than this. For example, he might ask them to blink, nod or shrug instead.)

Time

1 minute

Number of people

10 to 1,000

In advance

You'll need to give each audience member a flag or piece of card in a different colour.

There is one downside to any colour-coded voting system, because as many as 8% of men and 0.5% of women with North European ancestry are red / green colour-blind (according to the National Eye Institute).

For that reason, I suggest combining images or words with the colours. Obviously, you should choose an image or message that suits your topic.

One speaker I saw pre-prepares laminated cards that are green on one side and red on the other, with the words 'Yes' and 'No' overprinted. It's then easy for everyone to see the audience response when he asks them a question.

Running the exercise

At the appropriate moment in your talk, ask your question and invite the audience to respond by waving the appropriate colour flag or card in the air.

During the exercise

People may hesitate, and look around to see what everyone else has voted to assess whether their own answer is in line with the majority or not.

Calling this out can be a learning point if it fits with your talk topic.

After the exercise

Comment on the perceived percentage response that everyone has witnessed.

Adapt the rest of your talk based on the audience contribution. You've asked them to do something, so you have to let them know their response has been valuable, worthwhile, and is shaping what happens next.

Variations

For three-way voting, I invested in a few packs of coloured pipe cleaners. I sorted them into red, amber and green, and distributed them to the audience so each person had one of each colour. I call this 'traffic light voting'.

David Gouthro uses A4 paper preprinted with red, amber and green panels. One of the questions he asks is "Show me the colour that indicates whether the pace of this session is OK for you". Alternatively, you could design the page with three different black symbols, to take account of colour-blindness.

This photo shows the audience using this technique at the CAPS convention in Vancouver 2018.

Comments

Networking strategy speaker, Andy Lopata, asked me to devise a creative way he could capture audience answers to a series of questions he planned to ask a room of about 200 people.

We decided on the idea of distributing pieces of different coloured card to everyone's table during the break before his talk.

At the relevant time, Andy asked them to wave the appropriate coloured card in the air depending on their response.

It worked so well in making a clear point in colourful style that, after his talk, Andy told me at least three audience members came up to him to say they were going to use a similar approach themselves in future.

Not ideal for Andy as he was looking for something unique and memorable. If everyone else does the same, he runs the risk of looking as though he is copying **them** when he runs the exercise in future.

Binary decision-making

Depending on the seriousness of your question, you might want to give your audience three options instead of two.

Internet psychologist, Graham Jones, explains why binary choices give human beings a challenge:

There is considerable research on the psychology of choice and human decision-making. Even though all choices eventually come down to a selection between two things, the psychological evidence shows that human beings are really bad at making such a choice.

The studies show that humans are not good at choosing between several different things and we are pretty much useless at deciding between two different things. We are only any good at making binary decisions when the two things we have to choose between are similar.

Instead of trying to decide between two different things, you can find a way out of a deadlock decision by introducing a third option which is similar to the existing elements.

Source

Red / green voting is a simple idea, and here's one of the many places where I got it.

As a member of the PSA, I used to receive a monthly CD from the National Speakers Association (NSA) in America. It was a series of interviews with professional speakers called Voices of Experience, and it inspired lots of interesting ideas. I used to play it in the car because that's the only place I had a CD player. (VoE is now delivered via an app.)

One speaker told how he uses four coloured flags when presenting to audiences of 1,000 or more. The flags are bound with elastic bands and hidden under the table until the appropriate point in his presentation. This allows him to do a four-way vote. The cleverest element of this idea is that he thanks the audience for kindly wrapping up the flags back in their elastic bands after the exercise. They always do – and it saves him from sitting in a hotel room later, sorting out thousands of flags into sets of four.

To my shame, I can't remember the name of the speaker who told that story.

The public voting idea is also inspired by TV shows.

For example, on *Ready Steady Cook*, the audience votes by holding up an image of a green pepper or a red tomato. On the companion program to *The Apprentice*, the audience votes by holding up a sign marked 'hired' (green) or 'fired' (red). And on the lunchtime chat show *Loose Women*, the audience holds up a two-sided 'Yes / No' paddle.

Watch the video

http://tinyurl.com/XPRedGreen

Miscellaneous

These activities don't fit snugly into any other section. The reason they are hard to categorise is because they can be used in so many ways.

For example, the paper-tearing exercise works really well to make a point about communication, or diversity, or compliance, while the game mashup can be used as a revision exercise or just a bit of fun.

Of course many speakers have their own tried-and-tested activities with no input from me. You'll discover some of those in this section too.

In this section

- Envelopes
- Fun with cards
- Paper-tearing
- Game mashup
- Change chairs
- Timeline
- Pick a card, any card
- Woolly handcuffs

Envelopes

Overview

This simple idea creates a massive amount of anticipation, curiosity and intrigue.

Time

30 seconds (plus preparation time)

Number of people

10 to 100

In advance

Put all your little props inside separate envelopes (perhaps along with any handouts you're using). On the front of the envelopes, write 'Do not open until advised'.

Ensure the envelopes are distributed on people's chairs / tables before your session is due.

Running the exercise

At the appropriate time, tell the audience to find and open their envelopes.

As mentioned before, most people are obedient. They won't open the envelope until you say so. To be honest, it won't matter if they do take a sneak peek before you tell them to, because the items they find inside won't mean anything to them until you give the relevant instructions.

After the exercise

You might ask people how they felt when they saw the envelope, and whether they were compelled to obey (or disobey) the written instruction.

Variations

I once put envelopes on seats that contained no more than a branded 'thank you' card. I'll be honest. This was because I had some leftover cards and wasn't sure what else to do with them.

It was a nice quality coloured card in a square shape with the smiley face from my logo on the front and the words 'Thank you' printed inside in big friendly letters. The back had my contact details.

The result was astonishing.

People were interested to open the envelopes as soon as they sat down, and at least one of them contacted me after the talk to tell me I was a "classy lady" and to ask me to quote for some copywriting.

This simple idea turned out to generate a greater ROI than giving away expensive goody bags or printing promotional literature.

Action planning

There's no point in audiences attending your course or talk unless something changes for them as a result. And that usually means them taking some kind of action.

Unless you are responsible for implementation as well as instigation, you may never know what they do with the information you've given them. One way to incentivise this is to get someone else involved.

When I worked in corporate life, I was part of a peer-to-peer development group (now commonly known as masterminding). At the end of each session, each member would announce their action plans and we would appoint someone to be their 'conscience'. That person would phone them up after an agreed number of days to ensure they had done whatever they'd committed to.

After a training session, we often ask people to write an action plan. Maybe something as simple as listing their key takeaways, three ways they're going to behave differently, or what they will start, stop and continue doing as a result of the day.

Here is a powerful alternative.

If you want your delegates to remember their action plans, why not get them to write a letter to themselves instead?

An old-school letter in a handwritten envelope is a rare delight to receive. It stands out amongst the bills, and harks back to the pleasure we experienced in childhood when the only post we got was birthday cards and party invitations.

Case study

I went on a holistic holiday to Atsitsa on the Greek island of Skyros.

In the mornings, we might do open-air yoga before breakfast. Then we could study a course of our choice such as singing, improvised comedy or stained glass, before a communal lunch. There'd be a lovely long siesta, with time for a swim or reading in a hammock before the afternoon classes, then another shared meal followed by evening entertainment.

At the end of the fortnight, most people had relaxed, learned something new, and perhaps changed their outlook.

We were invited to write a letter to our future selves, to be posted back to us in three months' time.

As I wrote mine, I was thinking: "What's the point? I bet I remember I've written this."

But, sure enough, when my letter eventually turned up at home, it arrived as a complete surprise. It was a delightful reminder of an amazing holiday and the promises I'd made myself.

The Skyros holiday company have tried and tested this idea over many years, and worked out this is the most effective way to nudge people into sticking to their goals.

Source

I think the 'do not open' idea came out of my own head. Anyway, I don't remember seeing anyone else doing it.

Watch the video

http://tinyurl.com/XPEnvelopes

Fun with cards

There are lots of things you can do with cheap and cheerful index cards that help people to remember information more easily.

Sorting exercise 1

On the Copywriting for Recruitment masterclass I run with Mitch Sullivan, we wanted delegates to understand why people leave jobs – because the starting point for writing a good ad is to (metaphorically) put yourself in the shoes of your reader. To achieve this, we reveal the top seven reasons discovered in research done by recruiter, Jan Tegze.

In advance, I've prepared four envelopes, each containing seven cards, each card with one of Tegze's reasons written on. (I use a different coloured pen to write each set of reasons and label the matching envelopes so it's easier to sort them out afterwards.)

We ask delegates to work in small groups and sort the cards into the order they think was the most popular finding in the research. It only takes a few minutes, and they are always keen to know whether they've got the correct order.

As it happens, there is no 'right' answer, so whether they agree or disagree with the actual results, it leads to an interesting discussion. The point of the sorting exercise is that they are much more committed to knowing the answer than they would be if we simply gave them the data.

Sorting exercise 2

I was training an in-house comms team who were a completely different demographic to their customer base.

Before the course, I had interviewed some of their customers, and written selected quotes on index cards. I also made up some things that their customers would never say, and wrote those on cards too.

I divided my delegates into two groups, and gave each group a mixed pile of cards to sort out.

Their task was to identify which quotes were true and which were false, and then present their guesses to the other group before I revealed whether or not they were correct.

This sorting exercise worked really well as an engaging way of getting them to understand their customers' psyche. They were amazed (and amused) to find out how their customers truly thought, and now have the insights to serve them better in future.

Sorting exercise 3

As a copywriter, I often talk about taking a 'top down' or 'bottom up' approach. (Top down is when you write from the point of view of the company, while bottom up is writing from the customer's perspective – as mentioned on page 166.)

For one client, I prepared a set of index cards with snippets of their own top-down and bottom-up copy, mixed up the cards, and asked the delegates to sort them into two piles.

It was a good way of checking their understanding of the concept, using their own copy.

Inspiring creativity

I've used index cards to help delegates think from a different perspective.

For example, when working on taglines (as part of a marketing course), I ask them to pick a card and describe their business to the person written on the card e.g.

- *Five-year-old child*
- *Richard Branson*
- *Alien*
- *Your mother*
- *Competitor*
- *Your boss*
- *The Queen*

Similarly, I've asked in-house HR professionals to write an ad for a job that's outside their usual scope e.g.

- *Pizza delivery person*
- *Lady Gaga*
- *The Prime Minister*
- *Your pet dog / cat / fish*
- *James Bond*
- *Toilet attendant*
- *Your own job*

This helps unleash their creativity because they are released from their usual conventions.

Discussion prompts

On a marketing course I used to run regularly, I facilitated a PEST analysis prior to doing a SWOT analysis.

> PEST = Political, Economic, Socio-cultural, Technological
> It's a way of looking at the external context the organisation operates within
>
> SWOT = Strengths, Weaknesses, Opportunities, Threats
> It's a way of looking at the company itself, to help build its marketing position and strategy

Each analysis involves asking a series of questions. Rather than work through them all, I wrote the questions on cards and handed out one each. Here are a few examples:

- *P: What's the Government's current position on marketing ethics?*
- *E: Will interest rates have an impact?*
- *S: Will green issues affect your business?*
- *T: Can technology improve your processes?*

This creates a more interesting way to hold a discussion, and gives the delegates the chance to experience that way of thinking prior to going back to their office where they can answer the rest of the questions with their team.

Emphasis

I saw Caroline Hinkes give a talk where she got seven volunteers from the audience to stand at the front and read out a line from a card. Each person had to stress the highlighted word in the same sentence:

- **I** didn't say I stole the cookie
  No, someone else said it

- I **didn't** say I stole the cookie
  No, you said something else entirely

- I didn't **say** I stole the cookie
  No, but you probably did steal it

- I didn't say **I** stole the cookie
  No, someone else stole it

- I didn't say I **stole** the cookie
  No, you only borrowed it

- I didn't say I stole **the** cookie
  No, you stole a different cookie

- I didn't say I stole the **cookie**
  No, you stole something else

The point of the exercise was to show easily how the written word can be mis-interpreted.

Printed cards

Rather than rough-and-ready handwriting, you can use cards that are pre-printed with your instructions, a top tip, or a big image.

About 15 years ago, I was given a box of small cards by a training company. It's so nice that I've kept it all this time. One side shows their programme name (white on blue). The other is a positive word (blue on white) e.g.

- *Hopeful*
- *Charismatic*
- *Trusting*
- *Energetic*
- *Feisty*

These little cards can be dealt out and used to trigger all kinds of conversations – as part of a leadership programme, for example.

Most printers will be able to produce a set of business cards for you with different content on the back of each card – they don't cost much. All you need to do is decide what you want the cards to say.

On the subject of business cards, if we meet and you ask me about this book, I'll give you my four-page portrait-format business card. It looks like a mini-book, with the front and back cover opening out to reveal information and contact details inside. In that way, even the business card is interactive, engaging, and congruent with my message about being experiential. (That idea was inspired by marketing speaker, Geoff Ramm.)

You can buy a ready-made card deck from Kickitin.com that contains photos you can use to inspire conversations about leadership and other topics. For example, you can ask people to pick a card that represents a strength they have, or one they'd like to develop.

This is similar to a discussion exercise run by Susie Self, who leads a choir I sing in. Every time we get together, she asks us to pick an angel card – each card has a picture of an angel and a positive quality such as 'imagination'. Sometimes she uses Osho tarot cards instead. We then share whatever comes up for us with the group.

It's optional. No-one is forced into participating. But it's an interesting way of enabling us to check in with ourselves, catch up with each other, and focus on where we're at before we start singing.

Q&A

Another option is to give out blank cards to the audience to write their questions on. You can then gather the cards in, shuffle them, and give your answers in random order. This is just one of David Gouthro's suggested ways to enliven your Q&A session.

Sometimes he deals out playing cards and asks the audience to form groups by finding people who have the same suit, or matching pairs, or by teaming up to make the best poker hand. (For the latter, you'd have to explain the rules first.) You can also use this approach to invite questions from anyone holding a 6, for example.

Paper tearing

Overview

As George Bernard Shaw said, the single biggest problem with communication is the illusion that it has taken place.

I often use the paper-tearing exercise as a memorable way to embed the message that the responsibility of successful communication lies with the communicator not the listener.

You can also use it to draw out many other lessons. For example, a diversity message i.e. all people are different and that's OK. Or for sales teams, to demonstrate that face-to-face meetings are more likely to succeed than phone or email conversations.

Time

About 5 minutes plus any debriefing you choose to do

Number of people

2 to 1,000+

In advance

Each attendee will need a blank piece of A4 paper.

You don't want to use paper that is too thick, such as cartridge paper or card. A paper with a weight of 60 to 100gsm is fine.

That's the type of paper you probably use in your desktop printer.

Warn the organiser that you are doing a paper-tearing exercise, and that there might be a little bit of clearing up to do afterwards. In my experience, no-one has ever objected, but it's probably best to check in advance that they are OK with this. They might want you to describe the exercise and the learning outcome before they agree.

You will also need a £10 note (or other prize of your choice).

Running the exercise

Tell the people they will need their blank piece of A4 paper. (You might need a helper to hand out spare paper if anyone has already used their page to make notes.)

You will no doubt notice that some people start reaching for a pen. Tell them that they won't need one. You can do this in a fun and jokey way, or as a learning point. For example, you could discuss the danger of making assumptions. This already shakes up the expectations of the audience, because they know that usually when they are asked to work with paper they will need a pen.

If anyone questions it, you can say something like: "We're going to do an Origami paper-tearing exercise – I bet you weren't expecting that today!"

You will also need a blank piece of paper yourself. Hold it up in front of you so it is displayed in a way that the audience can see you are about to do the same thing as them.

When they all have their piece of paper ready, tell them to shut their eyes.

Some people will do this unquestioningly, while others will keep their eyes open.

This is another opportunity to interact with those people. Tell them you can see their eyes are open and repeat your instruction that for the next couple of minutes they will need their eyes shut. If you know them, use their names (teasingly) as you ask them again to close their eyes e.g. "Linda, I can see you, close your eyes please! Yes, Steve, that means you too..."

Reassure them all (perhaps laughingly) that they can trust you, there's nothing to worry about, and nothing bad or dangerous is going to happen.

Usually, this small amount of reassurance is all that they need, and even the most recalcitrant audience members will close their eyes.

If it **still** doesn't work, you could try waving your £10 note at them and tell them there is a chance to win it – but they need their eyes closed first.

In the worst-case scenario, some audience members might flatly refuse to shut their eyes. In that case, turn your back to the audience to conceal exactly what you are doing from those who are peeping. This is not because you're cheating, but because it could give them an unfair advantage. The exercise will still work, although you might need to peek over your shoulder from time to time to check how the rest of the audience are getting along.

I keep the turn-my-back idea 'up my sleeve' just in case, although I have never actually had to do this. I find that most audiences are incredibly obedient and will indeed to close their eyes on request. However, as with all audience participation exercises, you have to be ready for anything.

If you have any really reluctant audience members, you can ask them to look down into their lap rather than closing their eyes.

The only exception is when there's a lip-reader in the audience. In that case, you should obviously let them know they can keep their eyes open so they can follow your instructions.

During the exercise

When they all have their eyes shut (or they're looking down), tell them: "Now, with your eyes shut, fold your piece of paper in half."

Watch as they follow your instruction, and do the same thing with your piece of paper. Fold your page in either direction you like, width-ways or long-ways, it doesn't matter which you choose.

Interestingly, no audience member has ever interrupted to ask me which way they should fold it, and I have done this exercise dozens of times – maybe even hundreds – with many different groups.

To keep the pace up, you can say something like: "Let's do this really quickly." This also discourages interruptions and questions. The reason you want to discourage questions is so you can make a point about that later.

As soon as you can see that most (or all) people have folded their pages, tell them to tear off a little piece of paper in the top right hand corner, still with their eyes shut.

Do the same thing yourself. Throw your little piece of torn-off paper on the floor or table. Tell them it's OK to throw their torn-off piece away. Observe the audience as they do this.

It doesn't take long. As soon as they appear ready, tell them to fold their piece of paper in half a second time and tear off another little piece in the top right hand corner. Remind them to keep their eyes shut as they do it.

Do the same thing with your own piece of paper. It doesn't matter which way you fold the paper, which way you turn it, which corner you choose as 'top right', nor how big the corner is that you tear off.

Next, tell them: "Still with your eyes shut, fold the piece of paper a third time, and tear off another little piece in the top right corner."

Do the same thing yourself.

Then say: "Keeping your eyes shut, fold the paper in half a fourth time, and tear off another piece in the top right hand corner."

I sometimes add a comment such as: "Ooh, if you are anything like me, you might find it's getting a bit more difficult now; you might need your teeth to help you."

Observe as the audience follows your instructions. When you notice they have all (or almost all) done it, say: "When you have done this, open your eyes, open the paper – and if you have exactly the same as me, I will give you £10!"

Watch as they open their pages. Open yours at the same time and hold it up in a way that they can all see.

There is only a tiny chance that someone will have exactly the same as you.

After repeating this exercise many, many times, I can only think of two occasions where I have had to give away the £10.

Ask them to hold their pages above their heads so the rest of the audience can see too. (By the way, when everyone is holding their page in the air, it's a great photo opportunity.)

Comment on any particularly unusual or striking results – for example, some people have only a scrap of paper left, while others have almost a whole sheet with a few tiny holes. Allow the rest of the audience to chat about what they notice too. They will probably do this spontaneously anyway.

Tell them: "Look around the room. Can you see anyone else with exactly the same result as you?"

It is really unusual – even in a room full of many people – to find two pieces of paper that are identical.

If it happens, you can make a comment, perhaps speculating about the "crazy mind meld" that the pair have going on between them.

The reason that everyone comes up with a different result is because there are so many permutations about the direction the paper is folded, which corner is the 'top right', which way they turn the paper each time, and how big is the corner that's torn off.

It's amazing how many different results people produce. There are almost endless variations, and it's fascinating that each pattern is so unique. As mentioned above, I've only ever had to give away a prize a couple of times.

If anyone has matched your page, award the prize and instigate a round of applause for the winner.

If no-one has matched your page, make a happy joke about being able to keep your £10.

After the exercise

Take the opportunity to draw out the learning.

Praise them for obediently following your instructions. Tell them that most people have done their best to do exactly what was asked. If you as the speaker / trainer / presenter actually wanted them to produce the exact same result as you, they would have needed to see you and copy exactly what you did.

The lack of eye contact emulates a phone conversation. So, for a session about resolving conflict, this exercise could be used to show that face-to-face communication has the best chance of success.

If your talk is about diversity and acceptance, you can use it to explain that everyone interprets things their own way – and that nobody is 'wrong'.

For a team-building workshop, you could initiate a discussion about why people didn't ask questions if they weren't clear about the instructions. This would be a valuable way to give permission to teams who might sometimes need to challenge the brief they are given.

Example
Susannah Baum is former President of the Canadian Association of Professional Speaking (Montreal Chapter). She teaches people how to give presentations that have more structure, audience engagement and power.

She told me the paper-tearing exercise will reinforce her session on 'delivering your message'. Although she recommends a specific framework to follow that guides how people move and deliver their speech, she also tells them it's OK to be different. "Just because your way is not like someone else's, doesn't make your way any less cool or fun".

Variations

You can adapt this exercise by changing the number of folds, turns and tears you instruct the audience to do. You can repeat it with their eyes open, or by inviting questions, to show contrasting results. I'm sure you can think of your own twist too.

Comments

You can guarantee that people will remember the paper-tearing exercise days, weeks and even months later. I know, because I've tested it, as mentioned in the introduction to this book.

As a reminder, I re-visited a group of speakers 12 months after doing the paper-tearing activity with them, and asked for a show of hands if they were there and remembered the exercise. They did. I also asked if they could remember the point of the exercise. They could. Finally I asked if they could remember a single thing I'd said. They couldn't. I laughed, and said: "Neither can I!"

This is a simple demonstration of the power of interactive exercises on audience recall compared with their ability to remember your words and content.

Source

Sadly, I can't remember who demonstrated it, but I do remember that I first experienced the paper-tearing exercise at a business networking breakfast in a golf club in about 2002.

Watch the video

http://tinyurl.com/XPPaperTearing

Game mashup

Overview

This works as a good revision exercise, because it can help people learn key concepts, languages or vocabulary in a really fun way. Alternatively, you can use it as a memory test, or to draw out lessons about briefing.

Another learning point you could acknowledge is that everyone has different skillsets, which is why it's important to build a balanced team to get the best results.

In fact, you can adapt this game mashup to reinforce almost any message.

Include as many or few of the rounds as you please. Three is probably around right in a business context. Choose from the ideas below to find the ones that make sense for you.

Note that this is one of those games that takes longer to describe in writing than it does to play.

By the way, I've also heard it called 'The Hat Game' and 'The Bowl Game'.

Time

30 to 60 minutes (or more)

Number of people

Four to 20

In advance

You need a good-sized hat, bowl, or other receptacle, as well as plenty of plain paper and pens. Tear the paper into small pieces, each about 10cm x 15cm (that's A4 torn into eight equal pieces). You'll also need a timer that runs for 30 seconds.

With a smaller number of people, you play as individuals. With a bigger group, you'll need to break them into teams, ideally of equal numbers, although that doesn't matter too much.

Running the exercise

Give each person four pieces of paper. You could issue more, however, four is the minimum to ensure everyone gets at least one turn at every part of the game, since it's around the most guesses people can get right in 30 seconds.

Ask them to write the name of a **person** on their first piece of paper, as clearly as possible. They can choose anyone living or dead, real or fictional, or even a cartoon character, and it should be someone that everyone else in the game is likely to know. Examples:

- *King Henry VIII*
- *Madonna*
- *Donald Duck*

On the next piece of paper, everyone should write the name of a **place**. It doesn't have to be a country or landmark, it can be any physical place. As with all the categories, it should be somewhere the other players are likely to know. Examples:

- *Eiffel Tower*
- *The moon*
- *Inside your ear*

On the third piece of paper, they should write an **object**. Examples:

- *Pencil*
- *Cricket bat*
- *Kettle*

That might be enough, but you can add as many categories as you like. Here are some more ideas.

A **concept**. That is, a word that describes something that's not in the physical world (so you can't touch it). Examples:

- *Philosophy*
- *Thought*
- *Happiness*

A word they learned **recently**, or their **favourite** word of all time. Examples:

- *Mellifluous*
- *Juxtaposition*
- *Serendipity*

Any word of their choice. Examples:

- *Blue*
- *Chandelier*
- *Curlicue*

It doesn't matter if more than one person writes the same word or phrase.

The players should then fold each piece of paper in half (no more – this will make sense later) and put the folded paper in the hat or bowl. Once that's done, mix the pieces of paper around.

Nominate a time-keeper or take this role yourself, and set the timer for 30 seconds.

Playing the game

Now the game can start.

Pass the hat to the first player (or yourself).

At this point, you may or may not choose to share this top tip with the participants: "Listen carefully to the answers as they will be reused in every round."

Round 1

The first round is similar to the board game, *Articulate*.

Each player has 30 seconds to describe the word(s) on as many pieces of paper as they can within 30 seconds – without using the actual words that are written. The rest of their team / the other players have to guess the correct answer.

Note that each piece of paper has just one fold so it is quick and easy to open and read.

If any player wants to **pass** on a particular word / phrase, they can, and that piece of paper is refolded and goes back into the hat after their turn is over.

As soon as each word or phrase is guessed correctly, they keep that piece of paper for themselves or their team. If time remains, the same player picks another piece of folded paper from the hat. Depending on how well they do, it is possible to get through four or five in the time allowed.

The correct answers are collected by the player / team, any clues they 'passed' on are put back into the hat, and play moves to someone from the other team, or to the next player in line.

Eventually, **all** the pieces of paper will be answered – even the difficult ones. This happens because it's the people in the room who have written the words / phrases, and will eventually start shouting out the answers they know they wrote, even when they are not well described.

When the hat is empty, count all the pieces of paper won by each individual or team, make a note of the scores so far, refold all the papers and put them back in the hat.

Some people can take this round a bit seriously, but the game goes on to get funnier and funnier. Here's what happens next...

Round 2

This round is based on *Charades*.

Play continues exactly the same way as before, starting with whoever's turn was next at the end of round 1. This time, the players have to act out the word / phrase on the paper without using any words.

Because the words / phrases have already been identified once, the game gets a bit easier. Even when the acting is not at all relevant, laughter ensues as people start shouting out whatever they remember from the first round, whether that's the hardest answers, their favourites, or their own words.

At the end of this round, add up the scores once again, and put all the refolded papers back into the hat.

Round 3

Round 3 continues as before, but this time, players must make a single simple sound as a clue to the word or phrase on the paper.

People will probably complain that it's going to be too hard. I admit, it can be tricky, but it **is** possible.

For example, if the clue is 'Police', the player can make the repetitive 'nee-nar' sound of a siren. However, if the clue is 'London Bridge', you'll have to decide if players are allowed to hum the tune to 'London Bridge is falling down', or whether that counts as cheating because it makes it too easy. As the facilitator, you have to decide what you allow. Do this with a laugh and a light touch – remember, it's supposed to be fun!

What you will notice is that, when they can, people use sounds that literally reflect what's on the paper. They might also make a sound that other players used as clues in previous rounds. Either is fine.

For example, if the clue is Al Stewart, in the first round someone might say "He sang Year of the Cat'. In the second round, the player could act like a cat. In this round, the player might say 'Miaow', and the others will guess it.

Recognising the words or phrases from just a sound (and making it) is so challenging that it causes much entertainment. If you want an easier version, then allow people to give clues using just one word instead.

By this time, players should be getting fairly familiar with all the words in the game, however, you can keep adding as many rounds as you need. Here are some more ideas...

Round 4

This round is based on the board game *Pictionary*. (In my family, we call it *The Drawing Game.* One person makes a list, and we play it as a race between two teams.)

Players have to draw each clue for their team / the others to guess. No letters or symbols or talking allowed.

An A3 pad or blank A4 pages will work if the teams are small enough to gather round the drawings and see them clearly. For a big group, you may need to provide a flipchart that everyone can see. Ensure it has plenty of paper – and marker pens that work (I usually take my own as the pens provided by venues are often dried out).

Round 5

This round is called finger puppets. People have to act out the clues just using hand movements. No sound. No other body language.

It works even better if you've got access to a wooden chair with a slatted back. Put the chair on the table so people can put their hands through the hole from behind, using the seat as the 'stage' for their finger-puppet performance.

You'll have to be disciplined with your adjudication, as some of the clues will be really difficult to act out this way. Some people will no doubt try to pull faces or do a whole body charade rather than just using their hands.

Again, by this time, people are getting to know all the words and phrases quite well, so they will keep shouting out more guesses until they get it right.

Round 6

If you want to include yet another round, you can try facial expressions.

Players have to give the clues with their face alone. No sounds. No other movement.

Round 7

If you want to keep going, almost any game can be added using the same words. How about a round using modelling clay, for example? Or interpretive dance? What can you think of that will suit your goals?

Variations

To adapt this into a revision exercise, the categories you use can be based on your learning outcomes.

Ask participants to write (briefly) a topic they have learned in your session, a new word they have understood, or their main takeaway from the day. You will know what you want them to remember, so that's what you're trying to capture here.

The whole point is that people will have a far higher chance of remembering the words and phrases in the game, because they will have repeated them so often, and mentally processed them in so many different ways.

Comments

If you wish, you can rotate the role of time-keeper between all the players.

If you are playing and controlling the timer, keep an eye on it, or use a sound / vibration effect as well as the countdown clock. That's because it's very easy to get engrossed in the action and lose track of the time.

If you're playing the game as individuals (for fewer than eight people), all the others guess each player's clues. Each participant gathers the words they managed to guess correctly and counts them up at the end of each round to keep score.

This relies on people supporting each other and not sabotaging by deliberately failing to guess correctly. Some people might do this just because enjoy watching someone struggle. If it fits your theme, noting this tendency could lead to an interesting discussion afterwards.

Source

I was introduced to this game late one night at a Maydays improv retreat, and evolved it by playing it later with family and friends.

Watch the video

http://tinyurl.com/XPGameMashup

Change chairs

Benjamin Loh asked this question in the Speakers' Corner Facebook group.

Hello fellow speakers,

I'll be delivering a presentation to about 80+ senior executives and one of the themes is to embrace change as part of my content around Millennials engagement (yes, am one).

I know it's not exactly a concept that is ground-breaking, in fact, can be trite. Hence, I'm asking.

Has anyone run a group activity for such a crowd that is simple, interactive (not done alone) and can have them relate to the point / theme that change is often difficult, change is necessary etc.?

As part of the discussion that ensued, I suggested this:

If your session is after a break, discuss who sat in the same place as they did before, and why they chose to do that.

Either way, make them all stand up and move to sit on a different chair for the rest of the session.

Discuss how the upheaval made them feel.

Uncomfortable? Confused about the rationale? Fine in the new place after settling in?

Draw out the parallels with enforced change in the workplace and reinforce the learning.

Pam Burrows added her own version of the exercise:

I've run the 'change your seat' exercise repeatedly and it's so effective and energising. The following discussion on the learning points can last for ages!

I also add an unscheduled leaving of the room, taking pen and single piece of paper. No other instruction or explanation.

Outside, with nothing to lean on, they write their names with the opposite hand.

Once back inside, into a different chair, we have the discussion.

Communication, prior consultation, giving notice of change, having the right tools and support, all the analogies are there :)

Timeline

I learned about timeline therapy when I studied Neuro-Linguistic Programming (NLP).

> **Neuro** *for brain*
> **Linguistic** *for language*
> **Programming** *like computers*

I didn't do the course because I wanted to be an NLP Practitioner, but because I wanted to learn more about the power of words to influence behaviour, which is a close fit with my original career as a copywriter.

Timeline therapy assumes that people mentally position the past and the future in different physical directions. You can get them to stand at the point they consider the present, and then look (or walk) back to revisit their past selves, or forward to talk to their future self.

You can use this as a way to help participants to 'future pace' their action plans.

Timeline 1

Leadership and gravitas expert, Antoinette Dale Henderson, facilitated a timeline session to help our mastermind group with goal-setting.

She asked us to choose a spot in the room that felt like 'now', close our eyes, and point to where we imagined the future. Opening our eyes, we thought about our goal and took one step towards it.

Antoinette asked us in turn how much time had passed in our mind, and what actions we'd taken by then. She repeated this process until we'd each reached our goal – at least, in our imaginations.

Later, Annabel Kaye, one of the other attendees, was amazed to find she achieved her goal in real life a couple of months sooner than she'd predicted, and told Antoinette she thought the method was magic!

Timeline 2

When I was a senior manager, we used this method for project planning. All the stakeholders stood at one end of the room, which represented 'today'. We were invited to take one step forwards to indicate one week in the future, and then share whether we felt the project was still on track. We did.

We took another step forwards, which represented one month on. We were all still fairly happy that the project was going well at that point. After walking another couple of steps, we were asked to imagine we were three months into the project. One of the stakeholders admitted that something might be a bit wonky by then, but we were able to talk it out.

Three more steps along represented six to nine months later, and most of us felt the project had probably gone off the rails by then. This was based on our previous experience where we'd worked on projects that had been overtaken by other priorities and were never concluded.

The exercise helped us restructure what we planned to do and how we planned to do it.

Pick a card, any card

This information was written by Alan Stevens, and originally appeared in "The MediaCoach", his free weekly ezine, available at mediacoach.co.uk.

Here's a technique that I've been using for a few years to create a speech that is always unique and surprising, even to the person delivering it. I don't suggest using this on every occasion, and definitely not on a big stage, but for some audiences, in some circumstances, it can offer a refreshing change from the normal linear presentation.

It works for a speech or presentation where you are delivering several pieces of advice, several stories, or taking questions on various topics. Here's how it works:

- Take a pack of blank index cards
- Write a topic or story title on each of the cards
- Offer the cards, fanned out, to an audience member and ask them to pick one
- Take the card, read it, and talk about that topic for a few minutes
- Repeat until the end of your allotted time

Of course, you need to be able to talk about any of the subjects without further preparation. You should also ensure (as always) that all of the topics are of interest to the audience. I even made a video about the technique.

Watch the video

http://tinyurl.com/XPPickACard

Case study

I used Alan's idea when I delivered a speech to a network of landlords who wanted to know how to improve their ads on Spareroom.co.uk – that's the website that connects landlords with tenants. I was booked to give the same talk at two different regions, two days in a row.

The first time, there were about 30 people in the room, seated at big round tables. The second time, there were about 50 people seated theatre-style with a centre aisle.

I prepared a speech comprising my top ten tips. Each tip was backed up by a story, a drawing on the flipchart, or a live demo projected onto the big screen.

The 'pick a card' technique wasn't just a great way of engaging the audience as I walked around inviting different people to pick a card. It also kept me fresh, as the content was in a different order each time. Finally, it ensured I didn't forget anything, thinking I'd already said something on the second day when really I'd said it the day before.

At the end of my session, I divided the audience into groups and gave them each a different advert to analyse and report back. They loved the interactivity, as all the other presentations that day were straightforward talks with bullet point slides and graphs.

Finally, I issued a handout summarising the ten tips. Both presentations got rave reviews, and I was subsequently booked to speak at another three of their regions, as well as to create a video version of the presentation for their intranet, and to speak at their annual conference.

Woolly handcuffs

Gina Schreck speaks about social media marketing, and uses woolly handcuffs to embed a lesson about the need to think differently. She pre-prepares lengths of wool in various different colours, with a loop tied at each end, as shown below.

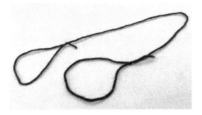

Gina invites participants to take a set of 'handcuffs' each. Then, she asks them to pair up, hooking the long piece of wool between them, and putting their hands through the loops (so each twosome is trapped together). Their task is to work out how to get untangled.

People will try all sorts of manoeuvres, such as dropping to the floor or attempting to wrap the wool over each other from behind.

The only way to escape is to put a loop from your hand inside a loop on the other person's hand, and pull it through.

Watch the video

http://tinyurl.com/XPWoollyHandcuffs

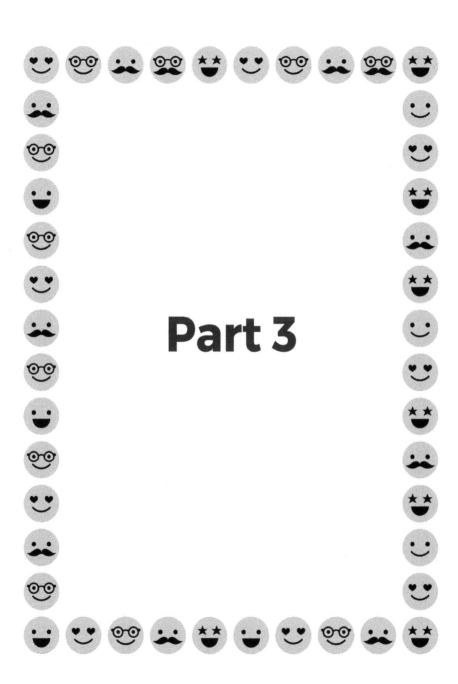

Part 3

Case studies

I'm sometimes approached to help speakers devise a breakout activity that is unique to them and their theme. This section includes a few examples that might inspire you.

In this section

- Speedy brainstorm
- Pop-up tent
- Rope trick

Speedy brainstorm

Andy Lopata was invited to work with the leadership team at HSBC in Hong Kong, and wanted a new activity to replace the mini-mastermind session he'd run with them before.

The objective was to demonstrate that a solution that works in one part of the business might be relevant to another. The desired outcome was that people would recognise that someone from outside their own department might have expertise that could be applied, and that no one should be 'written off' as a potential provider of a solution.

There were four tables of ten to 12 people each, and just ten minutes to run the exercise.

Andy's original idea was to ask each table to take two minutes to identify a shared challenge, and then eight minutes to go round the table with everyone offering solutions in turn. (This is unlike a traditional masterminding session where the group works on an individual's challenge and includes a Q&A to dig deeper into the problem.)

He contacted me to discuss it.

We were concerned that the tables would have to be self-facilitating, and that the timing might be tight. Some people might speak too much, while others wouldn't have the chance to contribute.

To collect maximum input and ensure that everyone could take part in such a short timescale, we agreed that the first two or three minutes could be spent identifying the shared challenge as originally planned. Then, rather than each person speaking in turn, I suggested that everyone should take five minutes to write their solutions on separate sticky notes to be stuck on a flipchart beside each table. The final couple of minutes could be spent gathered round the flipchart, to organise the sticky notes into similar groups and pick out the best ideas. Finally, maybe everyone could then take a photo on their smartphone so they have a record of their work.

Andy agreed that this would add energy into the activity while reducing the risks, and thanked me for being his 'go-to' creative person.

What happened

Andy told me he's now done this activity with several audiences. He said: "Thanks for helping me to come up with a new exercise to engage the audience. It worked brilliantly and really got people involved".

Source

The idea was inspired by a session I saw run by Shirley Taylor, former President of the Global Speakers' Federation.

Barnaby Wynter told me it's his favourite technique. He has used it in his Value Proposition workshops for over 20 years, and jokes that he's used so many Post-it notes that he should have shares in 3M!

I remember doing something similar when I was in corporate life, when guest trainers asked us to write down who we worked for. When all the sticky notes were collated, some people had written the name of their boss, some the name of the department, others the name of the company, and the rest the name of the parent company. The trainers said they were amazed because they'd never got such a variety of responses before. It revealed a level of confusion which we were then able to discuss and clarify.

Pop-up tent

A speaker from the Far East was referred to me. He is an explorer and adventurer who has climbed Kilimanjaro and tracked across the Arctic. However, his breakout sessions involve the audience writing on bits of A4 paper, which isn't congruent with the level of excitement, inspiration and adventure that's included in his talk.

After discussing his usual clients and their needs, we came up with a new idea that will be unique to him.

I suggested that he invite the senior leadership team on stage with him, and task them with putting up a pop-up tent. We all know how tricky it is to fold those things away, so he could add to the challenge by asking them to put it back in the bag again.

The exercise could be used to draw out lessons about leadership, teamwork, goal-setting, problem-solving – and you can probably think of a few more.

To further increase the level of difficulty, he could ask them to do it while wearing sunglasses and padded gloves – which would probably be the case if they were doing it on a real expedition.

He could even ask one to wear a blindfold, another to wear headphones, and another to tie a rolled bandana around their face, covering their mouth. That would become an interesting communication exercise, with one not able to see, another unable to hear, and the third unable to speak.

Imagine the impact on the watching audience when they see their senior leaders struggling to complete the task! And imagine their delight if / when the leaders succeed!

Of course, something like this would need to be agreed with the volunteers in advance. But, as an experience, it would be about a million times more memorable than writing on a piece of paper as audiences are asked to do all over the world every day. Let's face it, most of those pieces of paper end up in a file or the recycling bin, with the content completely and immediately forgotten.

Rope trick

Julie Holmes was speaking at the same event as me in Glasgow. She was planning an activity for an audience of 200 salespeople in the near future, and asked me to help simplify it.

She was talking about how the customer view of any brand is affected by what they experience during their buying journey.

She wanted to recreate a giant line graph using a long rope held up by volunteers. At first, she thought they might all stand in a row at the back of the room, holding the rope at shoulder height. The other audience members would get each volunteer in turn to raise or lower their section of rope according to what stage the campaign was at, as Julie described it.

The visual aspect of this exercise would clearly highlight where the customer experience fell short.

Julie would then challenge them to identify innovations they could undertake at that point. The volunteers would then lift their section of rope to reflect a more positive and continuous customer experience.

When she and I discussed this plan, we were concerned about the physical strain of having to hold a rope at shoulder height or above for a period of time, that the room layout might not be conducive to the exercise, and finally, that not everyone would be equally involved. A big rope would also be heavy for Julie to carry to and from the event.

Instead, I suggested every table having their own smaller rope they could use, while standing in a circle around their tables.

That way, each group would experience the exercise separately and be able to draw their own conclusions.

What happened

Julie had help from her mastermind group as well as from me.

She ended up doing the activity as a demonstration because the room wasn't conducive for doing it around tables. She asked volunteers to hold the rope waist high on either end, and it worked well.

It was a good lesson in testing any new activities, and planning for all contingencies.

Conclusion

In the book *Hard Times* by Charles Dickens, children are portrayed as empty vessels to be filled with information. For years, that's what education has typically been like.

As an adult, I discovered the *Three Principles* understanding. This suggests that people will only learn what they are ready to learn. If you try to give them motivation, it only lasts while they are still in your company or reading your book. If you give them tips and tricks, they will only take on board the advice that they were almost ready to realise for themselves anyway.

My client, Rose Padfield, also introduced me to nudge theory – that's the idea that you can't force people to do what you want, but you can nudge them in the direction you want them to go.

Thank you for being ready, willing and open to trying the ideas in this book.

Other experiential speakers

Obviously, I'm not the only person in the world who thinks there is an opportunity for speakers, trainers, facilitators and presenters to use activities that inject more audience engagement. Here are a few other examples and resources:

David Gouthro is a keynote speaker, event facilitator and MC (emcee) who believes in making his presentations as interactive as possible.

He says "I don't believe personal or organizational change comes about unless meeting participants are more engaged than simply remaining quiet and erect in their chairs while someone offers his or her sage-like advice from the stage."

When we met in Canada, David demonstrated some of the physical metaphors he uses that audiences find extremely powerful. For example, you can ask people to hold hands in a circuit to light up an energy stick or energy ball (search Google to buy them). When one link breaks, the light goes out.

David also introduced me to Liberating Structures – a website and app that suggests 33 microstructures designed to replace traditional presentations, discussions, status reports and brainstorms, and therefore help unleash a culture of innovation that boosts organisational results.

In the foreword he kindly wrote for this book, David mentions the Thiagi Group. They have compiled hundreds of interactive training games and puzzles to help participants laugh and learn.

Because learning can be accelerated through games, Clinton Swaine of Frontier Trainings uses game-based play to teach business and success principles in a fun way. He describes the company as 'the world leader in experiential business training'.

Bob Parker is another expert in experiential learning. He helps build high-performing cultures with The Pit Crew Challenge. Teams work as a pit crew and benefit from various outcomes, including how to collaborate, break down silos, and focus on the customer. At the time of writing, over 18,000 people have been through the program since 2001.

Bob says: "When done right, a shared experience creates engagement and alignment."

I agree – although my ideas are a lot simpler, with minimal props and preparation so they are accessible to all.

Playfulness

I was musing over the reasons why these activities work so well. I just know that they do. Then I realised. It's because they unleash the playful nature that all humans are born with.

Note that they're intended for adult business-people as they are my audience. I haven't tried them with schools, for example.

I told you I was an improv addict, and I did a 'train the trainer' session with comedy improvisation expert, John Cremer. In it, he explained how our schooling system is designed to churn out obedient corporate clones, and to educate the creativity and independence out of us.

By contrast, improvisation gives us permission to have fun, laugh and be spontaneous. It releases our playful side. This disrupts the formal expectations of business behaviour and standards, and leads to improved creativity and a happier experience of life.

Neuro-science supports this.

Dr Stuart Brown is the founder of the National Institute for Play. In his book *Play: How it shapes the brain, opens the imagination and invigorates the soul,* he claims that play is a biological drive that is as integral to our health as sleep or nutrition. It's essential for our social skills, adaptability, intelligence, creativity, problem-solving ability and more.

Dr Karyn Purvis of Texas Christian University says: "Scientists have recently determined that it takes approximately 400 repetitions to create a synapse in the brain – unless it is done with play, in which case it takes between ten and 20 repetitions".

If human physiology is fine-tuned for learning through play, then it makes sense for us to use games to teach.

Compliance

When you are the teacher, you can only teach when the pupils sit quietly in their chairs and listen. It only works as long as both parties play the role.

In the 1989 film *Dead Poets Society*, Robin Williams plays an inspirational teacher, John Keating. In one memorable scene, he says: "I stand upon my desk to remind yourself that we must constantly look at things in a different way."

He encourages his students to do the same, by each standing on his desk in turn.

At the end of the film (spoiler alert), Keating is fired from his job. When he leaves the classroom, the boys stand on their own desks to show they support him. It's a moving moment.

As a trainer or speaker, you are playing a role. It only works when the delegates sit quietly, listen to your expertise, make notes, and play their part.

But work and life are not separate. Work is part of life.

I left the corporate world to go freelance in 2001. One of the final projects I worked on was called Libra, because it was about work:life balance – a novel concept at that time. Today, with home-working, incessant emails and social media, the line is increasingly blurred, and the phrase has become ubiquitous.

Of course, we humans bring our personal attitudes and values into the workplace, and take home the stresses and strains of work.

But, when it comes down to it, nothing really matters. We don't have to play the roles that society has prescribed for us. Freedom lies outside those roles.

So why not make business more playful? Why not make your speeches, courses and workshops more fun? Why not play a game when it makes a point?

Your audiences still have to pay attention and participate, but it's in a really easy, fun way.

I hope this book has given you some inspiration to devise your own icebreakers and energisers to enliven your own talks and training sessions.

I've set up an Experiential Speaking group on Facebook – please join and share your adaptations and ideas.

> *"To stimulate creativity*
> *one must develop childlike inclination for play*
> *and the childlike desire for recognition."*
> ***Albert Einstein***

What next?

Want more ideas?

You'll find lots more icebreakers, energisers and games on the blog at ExperientialSpeaking.co.uk.

Please scroll down the homepage to sign up for updates sent direct to your inbox.

Want a unique breakout session, designed especially for you?

If you would like my help to devise a unique breakout activity that fits your theme, style and learning outcomes, please contact me to book a Skype or Zoom consultation.

Want to include an active networking session in your event?

You can book me to enliven your audience with networking games that help them get to know each other in a fun and creative way.

Run events for speakers and trainers?

You can book me to demonstrate any of these exercises in a fun and practical session to inspire your attendees.

Contact me at JackieBarrie.com

Acknowledgements

I can't take all the credit for the ideas in this book, and there are many people who have helped me along the way. I particularly appreciate the support of...

- Barnaby Wynter and Antoinette Dale Henderson who prompted me to write it in the first place
- My mastermind group(s) for their endless inspiration and encouragement
- Ade Cove, Kamile Kapel and Monika Ozdarska for the videos, and Neil Ben for editing them
- Alan Stevens and David Gouthro, for their kind endorsements in the forewords
- My friends and family, especially my Mum, for making me mad about games
- John Cremer, for introducing me to improvised comedy and unleashing my inner playfulness
- The team at AA Mac in Wallington, who valiantly tried to retrieve a lost day's work from a corrupted USB stick after I'd been working on this book remotely
- My sister, Rosemary Godfrey, for helping with Mac to PC glitches in the formatting (RosemaryHelpdesk.co.uk)
- George Chieza, Barnaby Wynter, Sylvia Plester-Silk and David Gouthro for their comments on the draft manuscript, and Tom Morley and Mike Clayton for advice on the cover. Their suggestions have made the book immeasurably better
- All my clients, trainees and audiences who have enthusiastically participated in the various exercises
- You, for reading it

About the author

As a copywriter, I help businesses and entrepreneurs to get their message across on paper, on screen, and face-to-face.

It could be by writing the words for their website, blog posts and printed marketing material, by crafting a core message they can use at networking events, or by helping to structure and clarify their presentation content.

As well as being a hands-on copywriter, I train business-owners, marketers and comms teams how to write compelling copy, recruiters how to write better job ads, and freelance journalists how to add copywriting to their skillset.

I travel the world, speaking about websites that work, identifying your core message, and effective communication skills.

I am increasingly being asked how to enliven a training session or speech with interactive icebreakers, energisers and audience participation exercises.

I hate tea, tomatoes and shoes, and like dancing, scuba diving and making people laugh.

ExperientialSpeaking.co.uk | JackieBarrie.com

Your notes